The Greatest Risk Of All

The Greatest Risk Of All

A Personal Testament of a Spiritual Quest to seek the Truth

Stanley Cohen

© *2012 by Stanley Cohen. All rights reserved.*

No part of this book may be reproduced, stored in a retrieval system, or transmitted by any means without the written permission of the author.

Contents

About The Book 1
Acknowledgement 3
For My Children 5
Prologue 7

Chapter I 9
Chapter II 13
Chapter III 15
Chapter IV 19
Chapter V 21
Chapter VI 25
Chapter VII 28
Chapter VIII 31
Chapter IX 34
Chapter X 37
Chapter XI 42
Chapter XII 45
Chapter XIII 49
Chapter XIV 51
Chapter XV 53
Chapter XVI 55
Chapter XVII 57
Chapter XVIII 58
Chapter XIX 60
Chapter XX 64
Chapter XXI 67
Chapter XXII 69

Chapter XXIII 71
Chapter XXIV 74
Chapter XXV 77
Chapter XXVI 79
Chapter XXVII 81
Chapter XXVIII 82
Chapter XXIX 85
Chapter XXX 90
Chapter XXXI 92
Chapter XXXII 96
Chapter XXXIII 98
Chapter XXXIV 100

What you are about to read is presented in the form of a novel, but, what is contained within this novel is real. This is a true story based on the life of Stanley Cohen. In most cases, not even the names of the people have been changed.

About The Book

I WOULD LIKE to introduce you to a novel about one man's journey to seek the truth about salvation.

The reader will be exposed to an aging Jewish man, raised in New York who now finds himself living in Russellville, Arkansas and coping with gut wrenching decisions he feels compelled to make concerning his faith. He is not alone in this spiritual quest as he is now in the company of a Christian Arkansas coalminer's daughter, who feels right at home in the "Bible Belt," and who is also open-minded to learn about Messianic Judaism and Yeshua (Jesus); the Messiah.

Our "hero" has been accustomed to taking risks all of his life and when he lost, money was involved. But, this is different. This would be his greatest risk of all . . . . for if he is wrong he could lose his soul.

Acknowledgement

TO

PAIGE

Who labored endlessly on this novel, making sure all the i's were dotted and the t's were crossed, and whose love and encouragement made this book possible.

For My Children

David

Danny & Nichola

Maria & Brian

Tommy

Jackie Faye & Bob

Greg & Debbie

Kelly & Margie

Douglas & Pam

Katie & Jeff

Carrie & Gregg

Prologue

How does one, now in his golden years, find the strength to change from one religion to another? Is it because of his fear of death? What would his dearly departed mother say to him? Would it mean that his ancestors, who perished in the holocaust, did so in vain? Or perhaps he now believes that the Lord has guided him on this new and strange path that would combine the best of Judaism with the best of Christianity and he would find Yeshua, leading to his salvation; If he has the courage to accept Messianic Judaism.

Chapter I

STANLEY COHEN, NOW age seventy two, listened intently to the Sunday morning service at the First Assembly of God Church in Russellville, Arkansas. He had attended this service sporadically; mostly because of respect for his wife and her family. But, this time was different.

As the service was drawing to a close, he started to sweat and he felt his heart beating like a drum in his chest as Pastor Ronnie Morris said, "Is there anyone here who has not yet accepted Jesus as your personal Savior and wants to now, please come forward." At that moment time stood still as Stanley reached back into his past.

* * *

Stanley was born in 1939 in Yonkers, New York to Louis Cohen, a plumber, and Ida Cohen, a homemaker. Ida attempted to raise Stanley and his older sister Doris, as Orthodox Jews. Louis, in his heart, was somewhere between a Conservative and Reformed Jew, but he followed Ida's more strict belief in the raising of their children.

Ida insisted that her son attend Hebrew school when he was ten years old. He attended Monday through Thursday immediately following public school from 3:30pm-5pm. This seriously cut into his playtime. He learned to speak Hebrew, not knowing what he was saying.

Stanley hated Hebrew school. Ida scolded him for playing "hooky" when she received form letters, "We missed Stanley in Hebrew school today. We hope he feels better soon and returns to school." She insisted that he attend Hebrew school to the age of thirteen to be prepared for his Bar Mitzvah (A Jewish ritual celebrating a boy's thirteenth birthday and his entry into the community of Judaism). But, age thirteen arrived and Stanley was definitely not prepared for his Bar Mitzvah.

*　*　*

Ida hired a Rabbi to prepare Stanley to learn his *Haftarah*(a series of selections from the book of the Prophets of the Bible that is publicly read in the Synagogues and acts as a part of the Bar Mitzvah when a boy reaches the age of thirteen), which he forgot the day after the Bar Mitzvah was over. His parents rejoiced with their family and friends as Stanley gave his Bar Mitzvah speech and then he sighed a big sigh of relief as his religious instruction had finally come to an end.

*　*　*

On the High Holy Days *Rosh Hashanah* (the Jewish New Year) and *Yom Kippur* (Day of Atonement, which is the Holiest day of the year for the Jewish people), the family attended services at Congregation Sons of Israel Synagogue which was within walking distance of their two-bedroom one-bath apartment. Stanley sat next to his father in the auditorium under the watchful eye of his mother, seated in the balcony as is the tradition for Orthodox Jewish women.

Since Louis and Stanley did not know when to sit or stand during the prayers, Louis would follow the actions of the congregation and nudge Stanley when to stand or sit. After a while, Louis would look at his watch, glance at Ida and say to Stanley, "Let's go," even though the services had not yet ended. They waited outside the Synagogue for Ida to finish praying.

*　*　*

One Saturday, Stanley accompanied his father to work. He and his father stopped at a local diner for lunch. When the waitress arrived to take their order, Louis ordered a ham sandwich on rye bread and a cup of coffee. Stanley, age fourteen turned to his father and said, "You are not suppose to eat ham, Dad." His father replied, "I like a good piece of ham once in a while and don't tell your mother."

Almost every Passover holiday his mother would invite all of their relatives to the *Seder* (which celebrated the exodus of the Jews from Egypt) and she would always compose something personal, in which she mentioned the persecution of the Jews during the Holocaust. She would become very emotional and Louis always comforted her.

Even though his mother was extremely strict, Stanley's father was very lax which resulted in Stanley leaning toward Conservative Judaism and away from Orthodox Judaism and beyond, but not quite Reformed Judaism.

* * *

Stanley graduated high school in 1957, received an Associate of Applied Science in apparel production and needle trade engineering from Fashion Institute of Technology and a Bachelor of Science in Business Administration from New York University. He served in the United States Army. He married a nice Jewish girl who gave him two sons, David and Danny.

At the beginning of his marriage, he joined a Reformed Jewish Temple where they did not wear the *yamika* (a round or diamond shaped "hat" that Jewish males wear to remind them of their faith in God who is higher than they are and beyond their comprehension) and prayer shawls. The complete service was entirely in English. He missed the tradition of wearing a *yamika* and not hearing some of the prayers in Hebrew, even though he could not understand them. He then changed to a Conservative Synagogue, though he rarely attended, and remained this way until his son David's Bar Mitzvah.

* * *

The marriage ended in divorce after twenty-nine years due to Stanley's excessive compulsive gambling.

A second marriage followed shortly thereafter that produced two daughters, Maria and Tommy and ended in a painful divorce resulting in Stanley's fear of never seeing his daughters again.

Stanley Cohen

* * *

Stanley earned a living by specializing in setting up sewing factories in foreign countries and training the management and staff to operate them.

At the time of his retirement, he was living and engaged in his profession in Puerto Rico.

Chapter II

PAIGE ENNIS, AGE 61, born in Hartford, Arkansas to George Brassfield, a coalminer, and Virgie Brassfield, a homemaker, was the youngest of eleven children. She was strongly raised Pentecostal and was taught that Jesus is the Son of God and the Messiah.

She graduated from Westark Junior College, Fort Smith, Arkansas with an Associate of Arts Degree, Bachelor of Science from University of Central Arkansas, Conway, Arkansas, Master of Science from Henderson State University, Arkadelphia, Arkansas and Master of Science from Arkansas Tech University, Russellville, Arkansas. She was employed as an elementary teacher and principal.

Paige was married to Jack Ennis forty-two years until his death in 2000. Their union produced six children (Jackie Faye, Gregory, Kelly, Douglas, Katie and Carrie) fourteen grandchildren and eight great-grandchildren. She was retired at the time of Jack's death.

* * *

In 2002 living in Russellville, Paige began to experience loneliness. She met Stanley, then age 63, online in a chat room called "romance 60+." Stanley lived in Puerto Rico. It was instant attraction via webcam for both Paige and Stanley. "What's your name?" asked Stanley. "Paige, and what's yours?" replied Paige.

For a split second he thought about how unhappy he was with his past and replied, "Scott," as if he was trying to recreate himself with the name of the main character of his first novel, <u>The Risk Taker</u>.

After days of chatting they exchanged phone numbers and their relationship added a new dimension as they could now hear each other's voice. Stanley fell in love with Paige's southern accent and she felt the same about his yankee accent. He soon sent her a copy of his first novel and told her that Scott was his nickname.

As their relationship blossomed, she invited him to visit her and her family for Christmas.

* * *

Paige muted the television when she heard the doorbell ring. She walked over to her front door and ushered in her son, Kelly and his wife Margie. "What are you watching on TV?" asked Margie. "Oh just some old movie that I've seen before," replied Paige as she turned off the TV. "Kelly, you look tired. Sit down." Kelly and Margie sat down and glanced at each other as though they were both waiting for the other to talk first. "We heard that you have been chatting with someone online." said Kelly. "So?" replied Paige. "He's from Puerto Rico and he's a JEW." "First of all, he's not Puerto Rican." He's white American born and raised in New York who's now working and living in Puerto Rico and . . . and . . . and what's the problem with his being Jewish? Jesus is a Jew," answered Paige.

With that, the doorbell rang. "Kelly, answer the door for me please." Her eldest son Greg entered the living room and sat down. "What are you talking about?" asked Greg. Kelly replied "What you and I were talking about earlier today." Greg continued, "Mother is it true that this man is a JEW?" "Yes, and are you ganging up on me now?" as Paige answered in a somewhat annoyed tone. "Well, you always wanted someone to go to church with you, mother, and he is not going to go with you. Why don't you meet someone here." added Greg. "I just don't understand how you can do this," chimed in Margie. Irritably, Paige said," Your father has been gone almost three years now and I've mourned enough and before you judge Scott," Scott? Who is Scott?" asked Greg. "That is his name and you are going to meet him over Christmas when he comes here to visit me, so hold your judgment until you've had a chance to get to know him."

CHAPTER III

"FASTEN YOUR SEATBELTS, we will soon be landing at the Little Rock Airport," said the flight attendant.

Scott exited the jet ramp with the nervousness of a 14 year old on his first date. As he made his way to the exit he ducked into the nearest men's room to wash his face, brush his teeth and comb his hair. Paige was waiting on the other side of security where they kissed and embraced for the first time.

At the time, both were unaware that Paige's daughter Katie and friend Annette had followed her to the airport and was watching her meet with this "online yankee predator."

* * *

When they arrived at Paige's home in Russellville, they were greeted by several of her children including Katie and Annette, who had arrived earlier to get a good look at their mother's "date." She introduced Stanley to them as Scott and the name forever stuck, except when he was in the presence of his sons, daughters and sister.

* * *

After the remaining "uninvited" guests left her home, she took Scott on a tour of her neatly landscaped three-bedroom, two-bath home with adjoining carport. He smiled to himself as he compared her nicely furnished cozy little palace to his one-bedroom, three story walk—up spartan apartment with cold tile floors and only one window air-conditioner. It was sparsely furnished and had one bath with the hot water being heated by a solar unit on the roof resulting in cold showers during cloudy weather. "Scott, could I get you something to eat and what would you like to drink?' "Later." he replied as he pulled her toward him and they looked into each other's eyes.

*   *   *

As the days passed, Scott was introduced to Paige's family, but could not remember all of their names. On the third day of his ten day visit, he noticed his novel, The Risk Taker, in her bookcase. He reached and pulled out his book and said "One of these days I would like to write a screenplay about this novel." "Have you ever written a screenplay before?" "No, but I have a couple of chapters of the screenplay Goodwill Hunting as a guide. You know fade in-fade out and all the other movie talk," continued Scott. "Why don't you write it?" asked Paige. "When?"he asked. "Right now. You can dictate it to me and we can start from there."

Paige's daughters Katie and Carrie helped with the typing and Katie created a cover for the screenplay based on The Risk Taker book.

*   *   *

The only break that was taken from working on the screenplay was Christmas Day. The entire family was present for Christmas dinner. Scott had told Paige that he loved the turkey drumsticks and as luck would have it, none of her family liked them.

At dinner one drumstick was placed by Scott's plate and the other saved. But, he filled up on white meat, leaving the drumstick laying there. After dinner, Carrie was helping to clean. She said, "Mom, can I take the drumsticks home to my dogs?" Paige believing that Scott evidently did not want them said, "Sure."

That night Scott began looking for his drumsticks. "What do you mean the dogs ate my drumsticks?" he asked. "I'm sorry," Paige replied as she hugged away his disappointment.

*   *   *

When the Christmas vacation was over, Paige drove Scott to the airport and they said goodbye at the security gate. Scott whispered in her ear, "I love you and I'll see you soon." She wiped her tears as she saw her new screenwriter walk through security.

Scott leaned back on his seat after take off clutching his copy of his screenplay, <u>The Risk Taker</u>.

Scott & Paige

Chapter IV

SCOTT AND PAIGE spoke on the phone and online everyday until the big day arrived. He had invited her to visit him in Puerto Rico in March. She visited her beauty salon, followed by a manicure and pedicure then packed and unpacked.... packed and unpacked.... and packed her luggage three times before deciding on her wardrobe.

* * *

"Are we there yet, Scott?" "Just one more floor baby," replied Scott. "So you live on the roof?" asked Paige, as she sighed when he finally opened the front door to his "luxurious penthouse pad." She tried to smile as he gave her the tour and turned on the lonely window air-conditioning unit.

His humble abode did not bother her as they were both happy during her two week stay, with him showing her the sites, his workplace and especially the house hunting as they were planning their future together.

* * *

Scott returned to Russellville and spent the July 4th holiday with Paige and her family and presented her with an engagement ring.

* * *

It was early August on a Sunday morning and as Paige walked out of her church, she thought how hot the weather was in Russellville and if it is this hot here, she could imagine how hot it was in Puerto Rico.

Her thoughts continued as she walked to the church parking lot, "I'm sure going to miss this church and my family when I join Scott in Puerto Rico."

* * *

Destiny took a hand in their wedding plans as Scott met his boss at the San Juan Airport in early August. His boss was based in their parent company in the United States and visited him in Puerto Rico twice a year.

As they drove from the airport to the factory, he learned that the United States parent company had decided to sell all of its U.S. holdings including this manufacturing plant in Puerto Rico and that they had at present three potential buyers that were biding and that the sale would be final at the end of August.

At the end of August they learned their fate as the buyer decided to phase out the entire Puerto Rico operation and that Scott would no longer be needed after mid-September.

* * *

Scott phoned Paige after learning when his last day of work would be. "Scott, that is wonderful. That means you can join me here in two weeks." "I was hoping to keep working until at least age sixty-five," he replied. "But, vocationally you don't have anything more to prove. You don't need to set up a new garment factory in 'tim buck two'. Honey, you've worked long enough. It's time to stop and smell the roses. It's time for you to retire and come home to me." "I know you're right; it's just that I've been active all of my life. You are going to need to teach me how to smell the roses." Paige sighed as they would now be starting their new life in Russellville.

Chapter V

THE WEDDING DATE was scheduled one week after Scott arrived in Russellville. The big day had arrived and he was at the Little Rock Airport to meet his sons and their girlfriends.

Carrie was styling Paige's hair. Jackie with her husband Bob, were picking up the wedding cake. Kelly and Margie offered to have the ceremony at their house and they along with Greg and Debbie and Doug and Pam were busy decorating for the wedding.

* * *

The time had finally come. The family, including Scott and the minister, gathered in the den for the ceremony. As Paige started to walk down the stairs to the den, her granddaughter Alison sang the "Wedding Song." Scott thought "How beautiful she looked."

David and Danny served as the Best Men, Paige's granddaughter Hanna was the flower girl, her grandson Nick was ring-bearer, Katie and Carrie were maids of honor, and two grandsons Tyler and Ryan were ushers with granddaughters Paige and Taylor tending the guest book. Before the ceremony began, Katie sang "When I Fall in Love."

* * *

The wedding was Christian with a Jewish ending as David placed a wedding glass wrapped in a white linen cloth under Scott's foot to be broken by stomping it. This is customary at Jewish weddings. Breaking of the glass has various interpretations of why they do this and where this wedding tradition came from. But, the most popular explanation is for a reminder of the destruction of the Temple in Jerusalem. When he broke the glass Debbie yelled *"Mazel Tov"*(congratulations).

After the last member of the family had gone home, Scott took his Mrs. Cohen on their honeymoon to Branson, Missouri.

Scott & Paige wedding photo

Scott & Paige with 8 children wedding photo

Chapter VI

THE HONEYMOON WAS over and Scott was living in *Paige's house* and driving *Paige's car*.

Although he honestly felt that the third one was definitely a charm and he could not have asked for a better mate, the city of Russellville, Arkansas, which is the county seat and largest city in Pope County with a population of 27,920, was closing in on him. He was educated in New York City and had traveled the world and could not imagine settling down in a city that had a total area of 28.3 square miles. Unfortunately at this point in time, he was not yet ready to appreciate the advantages of living in a small city. He was also unaware that it is the home of Arkansas Tech University and Arkansas Nuclear One, Arkansas' only nuclear power plant.

It would take Scott even more time to learn about the beauty of Lake Dardanelle as well as the Arkansas River which borders Russellville. The only thing that he knew at this time was that he and Paige needed to explore and find another place to live and according to mapquest, the Oklahoma border is approximately ninety miles west of Russellville and Little Rock, the capital of Arkansas, is approximately seventy-five miles east of Russellville. He also found that Memphis, Tennessee is approximately two-hundred and five miles east of Russellville.

When he thought about taking a ride to Oklahoma his memory slipped back to the time when he was a young man stationed in Ft. Sill, Oklahoma where he received his U.S. Army Artillery training and remembering Oklahoma's wide open plains. He quickly ruled out Oklahoma.

When he mentioned Little Rock to Paige she told him "I go to Little Rock often and there's no way that I could be happy there."

They packed some clothes for a few days and off they went to Memphis.

When they arrived in Memphis, Scott liked the cosmopolitan atmosphere of this city. But when he saw the negative expression on Paige's face, he knew that his coalminer's daughter bride was not "citified" enough to live there full time. So, they explored the suburbs of Memphis and accidently crossed the Mississippi border into Southaven, Mississippi. At least they had found an area that they both liked with its suburban living, friendly atmosphere and nearby Memphis.

They explored Southaven and Scott bought a local newspaper to see what was available for rent and/or purchase in the classifieds. When he became excited while looking at new two-bedroom apartments, Paige was engulfed with the fear of moving away from her family and church. She felt that if she expressed this fear to him, he might think she was over-reacting.

Their search for a new residence also led them to a nearby community called Horn Lake where Scott saw a sign advertising the Horseshoe Casino in Tunica, Mississippi. "How far is Tunica?" Scott inquired. "I think about ten to fifteen miles away."Paige replied. "Are you hungry?" Scott asked Paige."A little," she smiled. "Let's drive down there and have lunch."

Before they reached the Horseshoe, the first casino they saw was the Grand. Scott parked at the Casino. They walked through the casino listening to the constant ringing of the slot machines searching for the restaurant, when they passed an area marked 'poker' and displaying about fourteen poker tables all in action. Immediately Scott inquired of the nearest restroom. He barely made it in time to avoid an accident as the excitement of playing poker coupled with the memory of financial ruination caused him to have a bad case of diarrhea.

When he came out of the men's room he took Paige by the arm and said, "We passed a Bob Evans Restaurant in Southaven and I love their food. Let's eat there instead." Paige, who was well aware of Scott's past gambling problems smiled as they headed back toward Southaven. He didn't realize at that time that he'd won this battle.

During lunch Paige saw that Scott was in deep thought and she decided to leave him to his thoughts until he was ready to share them with her.

Eventually during dessert, Scott said, "This area is too dangerous for me to live; it's just a hop, skip, and a jump away from several casinos which is poison for me. I'm not saying that I will never play again, but I'm certainly not going to live on top of it and besides I don't think that you would be happy . . . . completely happy away from your family and your church. What I'd like to do is take a hotel room in Southaven for the night and in the morning drive back to Russellville as I have some ideas how we can improve our house. I'll show you when we get home."

* * *

Scott did not know that her prayers to Jesus had been answered.

Chapter VII

Several weeks had passed and Scott had slowly started to settle down in Russellville. He knew that he could not live for any extended period of time in *Paige's house* and he made a mental note to start house hunting for another home in Russellville. For now, he put that on the back burner. However, they purchased two recliners, desk with chair and converted one of the three-bedrooms into an office.

He was delighted how this room turned out. The walls were filled with his accomplishments and pictures of his family which gave him a sense of satisfaction and pride. This occupied him for only a period of time.

* * *

Since he was use to being involved in different projects such as setting up factories and researching what needed to be done to accomplish a beautiful piece of art, he began researching new cars to purchase just the right one. Scott and Paige used this time of driving from dealership to dealership to enjoy just being together and being involved in yet another new project.

* * *

The holidays were rapidly approaching and Scott was looking forward to his first Thanksgiving with Paige's family. Her entire family and some of their friends gathered at *Paige's house*. Before dinner was served, all of the men gathered around the carport to observe Scott and Paige's new car. After several moments of 'tire kicking' and examining the automatic climate control Paige interrupted them. "Come on, it's on the table. I don't want the turkey to get cold."

* * *

In the middle of the Thanksgiving dinner, Timothy Johnson, a long time friend of the family said, "How much did you pay for your new Ford, Scott?" "Twenty eight thousand five hundred," replied Scott. "Isn't that a little high for that model?" continued Timothy. "This car listed at just about thirty-two thousand but I took advantage of the factory rebate and did some research on the internet to see what the dealer really paid in order for me to have the price reduced with the dealer still making a profit," answered Scott. "I wish you would have taken me along when you bought it, I'm sure I could have 'Jewed them down' at least another one-thousand dollars," said Timothy. Scott's face flushed as his anger swelled within him. He opened his mouth to speak but decided against it. "I'm suppose to be among family and friends, how could he say that to me?" he thought. Paige noticed Scott's reaction and his back tightening; she grasped his hand and gently squeezed to calm him down.

* * *

After dinner, all of the men watched the football game as the women cleaned up. Katie whispered in Paige's ear. "Mom what's wrong with Pop, he got very quiet during dinner? Is anything wrong?" "I think it hurt him when Timothy used the 'Jew them down' expression. "Why Mom, what's so bad about that?" "You know that Scott is Jewish and it just hurt him," declared Paige. "But Mom everybody uses that expression and I'm sure Tim didn't say that to hurt him." "Scott is the first Jewish person that I know and I think he may be the first for the family and friends. Apparently this expression bothers him," Paige replied. "What do we do now?" Katie asked. Paige said, "You are very friendly with Tim's wife, Clara. Please talk to her and tell her to ask Tim to never use that expression again in Scott's presence and I'll make sure that the rest of the family knows."

* * *

That evening after everyone left and Scott and Paige were alone, Paige turned to him and said, "Honey, I'm sure that Timothy did not mean to hurt you." Paige I've heard this type of ignorance all of my life and I won't tolerate it in my own home," Paige wanted to tell Scott at that point that she too had used that expression because she had heard it her entire life and never meant it as slurring or slanderous; it was just an expression. She did not know until now that this expression was offensive to Jewish people. But, she decided to let Scott cool off for now.

Chapter VIII

CHRISTMAS WAS ONLY a few days away and Scott decided to accompany Paige to church. He nervously followed her down to her favorite pew and shook hands with the parishioners that she introduced to him. When her family joined them she smiled as to say, "See I told you so . . . . that he would attend church with me."

He scanned the inside of this beautiful very modern sanctuary. On the same level as the pulpit but on the far right just below the choir, was a band consisting of a piano, guitar, violin, horn, and drums. If one didn't know the words to the hymn the choir was singing, two large screens displayed the words on the left and right of the stage.

The band started to play and the choir joined in and everyone stood. Scott was impressed as he saw how devoted the congregation was as they stood with one or two hands extended up toward God.

The music came to an end and everyone sat down. Pastor Ronnie Morris approached the podium and gave his sermon. At one point during his sermon Scott heard a strange language coming from a member of the congregation that he could not identify followed by an English translation from another member of the congregation. He was to learn later that the unknown language was spoken in tongues and he was so sure at that time that this was staged.

* * *

When the service concluded Scott and Paige were joined by Greg, Debbie, Kelly, and Margie in the parking lot. Greg said, "How did you like church this morning?" "It was very nice," replied Scott. "You need to attend more often. You do want to be able to go to heaven with mother, don't you?" continued Greg. "I believe that as a Jew I'll still be able to go to heaven with your mom," said Scott. "The only way to get to heaven is thru Jesus Christ," said Greg. Scott smiled at Greg as he said," What restaurant are we going to for lunch?" hoping to change the subject.

* * *

After lunch Scott and Paige returned home and Scott went online to the Assembly of God website and learned that the Assembly of God believes:

(1) In the Bible as the inspired and infallible Word of God (2Timothy3:15-16).
(2) In one God, eternally existent in three persons: Father, Son, and Holy Spirit (Deuteronomy 6:4; Matthew 28:19; Mark 12: 29).
(3) In the virgin birth of Christ, His vicarious, atoning death, bodily resurrection, and ascension (Isaiah 7:14; Romans 8:34; Acts 1:10).
(4) In salvation through the blood of Jesus Christ (1John 5:10; Romans 10:13-15).
(5) In baptism by immersion (Matthew 29:19).
(6) In divine healing through the redemptive work of Christ on the cross (Isaiah 53:4; Matthew 8:16-17; James 5:14-16).
(7) In the baptism with the Holy Spirit with the initial evidence of speaking in other tongues (Acts 2:4; 10:44-46, 19:6).
(8) In the sanctifying power of the Holy Spirit which enables a believer to live a holy life (Hebrews 12:14; 1Peter 1:15-16).
(9) In the second coming of Jesus Christ (Acts24:15; Luke 14:14; Revelation 19:7-9).

He also learned from the Assemblies of God (USA) Official website and Wikipedia Free Encyclopedia that the Assembly of God is Pentecostal which places a special direct personal existence of God thru the baptism in the Holy Spirit. The term Pentecostal is derived from Pentecost; the Greek name for the Jewish *Feast of Weeks*. For Christians this event commemorates the Holy Spirit upon the followers of Jesus Christ as described in the book of Acts.

Pentecostalism is an umbrella term which includes a wide range of different cultures and theology. For example; many Pentecostals are Trinitarian and others are non Trinitarian. In the case of the Assembly of God, they are Trinitarian.

Currently the Assemblies of God USA and Assemblies of God Organizations around the world make up the world's largest Pentecostal denominations with some sixty-million members and adherents.

* * *

Scott was stunned and impressed to find that a kinship, that is a mutual respect, developed between Russellville's First Assembly of God and Judaism as they shared the same roots.

Chapter IX

IT WAS DECEMBER 24th morning and Paige was making breakfast for Katie, Carrie and Margie who were decorating the Christmas tree that her sons and son-in-law, Jeff had brought her the night before. The television was on and they were all listening to Christmas carols.

While Scott was seated in his recliner reading the newspaper and enjoying the Christmas music, he began to feel those old feelings of guilt that he experienced as a child hearing music that was playing in all of the businesses in Yonkers, New York. Since he was Jewish, he felt that he was not suppose to like Christmas music.

He also remembered that he was jealous that Christian children were receiving Christmas gifts on December 25th and he did not. It seemed to him that on Christmas Day he 'conveniently' forgot that his parents had given him gifts on the Jewish holiday *Hanukkah* (festival of lights). His thoughts of yesteryear also reminded him that Christmas was Paige's holiday and that he had not yet purchased her a gift.

* * *

Scott scanned the classifieds of the Courier, the Russellville local newspaper and his eyes focused on "pets for sale." He always had a thing for German Shepherds and Golden Retrievers. He found two ads; one for German Shepherd puppies and the other for Golden Retriever puppies. Without anyone noticing, he tore the pet section from the newspaper and put this in his pocket.

After breakfast was finished, he asked Carrie if she would ride with him to find the addresses of the puppies. As they went out the door,

Paige said "Where are you two going?" "I want to drive Carrie's new Infinity. I've never driven one before," replied Scott.

As they drove away from the house, he explained to Carrie the plan to get Paige either a German Shepherd or Golden Retriever puppy. Carrie immediately knew that her mom did not want a pet but replied, "Oh that'll be nice."

Scott first called the number for the German Shepherd, but received their answering machine. He then called the number for the Golden Retriever and someone answered. He was informed that the puppies were for sale for $50 each and that they would have been more expensive but they did not come with AKC papers. "I'm interested in buying a female as we have grandchildren and I think a female would be more compatible for them." "Come on over we do have some females left," replied the owner.

When they arrived at the address in nearby Dover, Arkansas, they were informed that all the females had been sold and only two male puppies were left. "Could we see them?" asked Carrie.

Scott and Carrie sat on the couch in the living room and the owner showed them the two remaining puppies. "Which one do you like, Pop?" asked Carrie. Scott replied, "I like the one on the left." "So do I." As they were holding and looking at the puppy, a very large male Golden Retriever entered the room. "This is their father, "The owner said. Scott stared at this 'horse' and thought, "My goodness, is it possible that this puppy will be as large as his father." "Can I pet him?" "Sure go ahead."

Scott carefully held his hand out toward the large dog, who slowly walked over to him and it was clear that this dog enjoyed human contact. "Wow, he is so big," remarked Scott as he petted the father. "He's about seventy-eight pounds." The owner said. Scott didn't know at this time that seventy-eight pounds was just a drop in the bucket compared to what was yet to come.

"We'll take him. This is a Christmas gift for my wife." "It's very cold outside. Do you have a blanket to wrap him in and a ribbon to put around his neck?" asked Carrie.

The puppy was wrapped in a baby blanket with a red ribbon around his neck and one day supply of dog food in a zipped bag. As Carrie drove home, Scott held the new member of the family in his arms.

* * *

When they reached home, the Christmas decorating crew had left and Scott having forgotten his key, knocked on the door holding the puppy in his arms. Paige opened the door and stared in shock as Scott said, "Merry Christmas, honey. This is Risky." She embraced her new puppy as she thought," I don't want this dog, but I just don't want to hurt Scott's feelings."

Chapter X

CHRISTMAS MORNING CAME unusually early for the Cohen's as they were abruptly awakened by a very scared Golden Retriever pup, who was confused by his new surroundings, a small cardboard box lined with his baby blanket, and who missed his biological mother.

As the morning progressed, Paige borrowed a 'crate' from Greg, which was a small cage, used to serve as a housebreaking tool for Risky. He hated to potty where he had to sleep and therefore; he became housebroken very quickly.

That day Risky was introduced to all of the family, especially the grandchildren who gathered there on Christmas Day. Everyone held him and fussed over him and when they left Scott picked him up and held him close to his chest. At that time Risky dug his claws into Scott's shirt making Scott aware that his new pup was afraid of heights.

For the next few weeks, during the day, Risky would always crawl under the living room sofa all the way to the back and nap. This seemed to be his way of letting everyone know that he did not want to be disturbed while sleeping. Paige and Scott were to learn that when he was too big to fit under the couch, he would hide his head under the living room drapes while sleeping and would feel secure that no one would see him even though the rest of his growing body was exposed.

Once a week Paige bathed Risky in the bathtub and always had to stop him from drinking the bath water. After his bath she placed him on the bathroom vanity and dried him with the hair dryer. He would hide his head under her arm as he did not like the sound of the dryer. He loved to come into the bathroom while Paige put on her make-up and sit and watch her.

* * *

The back door of the house opened onto a deck with a few steps leading down to the fenced back yard. One day Risky crawled under the deck to take a nap and, when he could not find his way out, he started to cry. Paige's granddaughter, Jennifer, then age fourteen, crawled under the deck and rescued him. After that episode they had a local carpenter install lattice around the deck to prevent this from happening again. When it rained and Risky begged to go out he would walk under the roof gutters to play and get soaking wet. When he came in Paige attempted to towel dry him, but to no avail, as his muddy footprints tracked throughout the house.

* * *

As he grew he doubled his size every month. Risky, if permitted, would always sit by Scott's chair and put his paw on Scott's knee when he wanted food from Scott's plate. Once Scott picked up his napkin and wiped his mouth and said, "All done, all done," Risky would go to Paige and start this scene all over again. When they left the dinner table he would then go over to his dish and eat his own food.

* * *

Risky loved when friends and family came to visit. The list also included UPS drivers, repairmen and all other human beings. He jumped on everyone who came into the house to receive their affection. When multiple members of the family were sitting in the living room, he would run from one to the other. As he grew larger this became a problem as some of the older members of the family feared being knocked down.

Scott and Paige tried to calm him down in front of visitors. It soon became apparent that the only way to have a quiet conversation with visitors was to put him in the backyard until they left.

* * *

Risky's shots were renewed at the age of one and every year thereafter. He grew to be huge and on his visit to the vet he would put his paws on the counter and look over at the receptionist who immediately knew that "Risky Cohen" was there.

When the vet told Scott that Risky was the largest male Golden Retriever he had treated and that he was overweight at one-hundred-twenty-three pounds, he was put on a diet of two and one half cups of dry dog food twice daily along with diet treats plus all the food he could beg, borrow and steal.

Golden Retrievers are said to have a long puppy-hood and as the years went by Risky proved to be no exception.

* * *

Risky's bark was very distinctive as to whether a family member or others came to the door. For a stranger his bark was very loud and sometimes the hair on his back would stand up. But, when a friend or family member approached the door he would whine and cry while beating his wagging tail very hard against any object in which he came in contact with. Paige and Scott often wondered if a burglar should come into their house, if Risky would protect them or assist the burglar in carrying out the contents in the house.

Taylor, their granddaughter, would lie on the floor by him and hug him. He would wrap both front paws around her and hug her close. He was truly a lover and not a fighter.

* * *

Scott often wondered if Risky understood the shows that were playing on television. The family liked the re-runs of the Andy Griffith show especially the episodes where the character Otis would get drunk, then, lock himself in jail.

One day Scott and Paige were looking for something online in their office when Risky entered and began to make a nuisance of himself. He would try to distract them from working on the computer by placing his toys on their lap and nibbling on their feet. When he was made to leave the office, he got angry and went into the living room and began tearing up a magazine. He then put himself in jail behind the coffee table as he always went there when he was in trouble.

Risky

Risky

Chapter XI

AS THE SEASONS passed, Scott began to settle in as a retired man living in Russellville, but he always looked for projects to keep him busy. Whenever one of Paige's children wanted to purchase an automobile he would spend endless hours online researching the vehicle and price.

He accompanied Paige to church occasionally and always tried to smile at Greg when he mentioned Scott's absence of Jesus and the threat of not entering heaven.

* * *

One Sunday night the Crabb Family, an evangelistic singing group, sang and ministered at Russellville First Assembly of God. Paige attended with Greg and Debbie.

After the service had concluded, Paige approached Jason Crabb and told him that her husband was Jewish and did not know or believe in Jesus. He took her by the hand and prayed asking Jesus to reveal himself to Scott, either in a dream or some way that he might believe and accept him into his heart and life.

Later that night, when she returned home from church service she did not mention the prayer for Scott who was occupied watching an old John Wayne western and playing with Risky. "Did you enjoy the service tonight, Paige?" "It was wonderful. I wish you could have heard them."

* * *

That night in a dream, Scott was standing next to the first step of a Christian church and watching well-dressed families walking in and appearing to be very happy and anticipating greater happiness once inside the church. "Why don't you go in?" asked a plain non-descriptive man who was standing on the third step. Scott answered "But I'm Jewish!!!" The man replied, "So am I." Then the dream ended.

* * *

The next morning Scott was sitting at the breakfast bar as Paige prepared breakfast, "I had a crazy dream last night. I was standing in front of a church and I don't know where or what kind of church specifically except it had a cross in front and I was watching people who looked to me like families . . . . mothers, fathers, and children who were greeting other families and everyone appeared to be happy as they were walking into the church.

Just then, this guy in his thirty's, plainly dressed and not wearing his Sunday best and standing alone above me on the third step said, "Why don't you go in?" I told him that I was Jewish. He answered, "So am I." Paige stopped what she was doing and questioned Scott. "What did his face look like?" "I don't know just a plain guy, nothing special." "What else did he say to you?" "Nothing, just what I told you." "Did he look foreign?" "I don't know, just a guy." "What did you do next?" "Nothing, the dream ended and I awakened." "Oh I see." "Remember I want the bacon crispy, but don't burn it. Why are you so interested in this dream?" "I was just curious." Paige felt a sense of awesomeness and experienced chills all over her.

* * *

During the day Paige wanted to tell Scott about the prayer with Jason Crabb but, she was afraid that he would not believe that this prayer happened or she was using his dream as her opportunity to promote Jesus.

* * *

That night she found the courage to approach Scott about the prayer and his dream. "Paige, are you making this up?" "No honestly I'm telling you that I talked with Jason, he prayed and then you had this dream." "Tell me the truth did your family put you up to this? Did you tell Greg about my dream? I bet it was Greg. Sure that's it. He is always pushing me to accept Jesus or I won't go to Heaven. Yea, that's it." "Look Scott, lying to you is not in my vocabulary especially when it comes to God and Jesus." "Well it is sure one heck of a coincidence that I would have this dream right after that prayer." "It's not a coincidence Scott. I believe this prayer was answered and Jesus appeared to you in your dream."

* * *

The next day Paige told her children about the prayer and the miracle of this dream. Her children were in awe.

When Scott thought about his dream incident, he could not explain it and that made him wonder.

Chapter XII

SCOTT KEPT WONDERING about his dream. Could this be Jesus who appeared to him? As he thought about this, he remembered that when he was very young (eight or nine) living with his parents in Yonkers New York, that the name Jesus was a sore subject.

One day when he was walking home from school accompanied by some of his "so called Christian friends", some of them began to taunt him saying "You killed Jesus." "No, I didn't." "Yes you did, all the Jews killed Jesus." When he reached home he was crying as he told his mother what had happened. "You didn't kill Jesus. You didn't kill anybody. Don't listen to those boys," said his mother, Ida.

This was not the last time that something like this happened. As he grew older and especially in his teenage years, he was taunted with the same ignorance, but this time he would answer them with his fist instead of running home to Ida. This type of anti Semitism eased up somewhat in his life when he entered college but was still present. The terms "Jew boy," "Hebe," "Moses" as well as "Christ killer" continued to make the hair stand up on his neck as the anger swelled within him. Even in the military, this type of anti Semitism was present, but less when the chips were down and everyone had to depend on each other.

* * *

He was now living in the "Bible Belt" and his guard was up, but this began to soften over time as Paige exposed him to the First Assembly Of God Church and Christian evangelical leaders such as John Hagee, who all favored the State of Israel as the "key" to the return of Jesus.

Stanley Cohen

* * *

Greg continued his acceptance of Jesus lectures, but one day Paige's son Kelly visited Scott at home and gave him a personalized copy of the King James Version of the Bible. It was presented by Kelly, Margie, Alison and Hanna. He also gave him some literature and said, "I would like for you to read this when you get a chance. I think you might find it interesting." He handed Scott <u>God's Covenant with Israel</u> by Rabbi Benyamin "Benny" Elon and <u>Y'Shua, The Jewish Way To Say Jesus</u> by Moyshe Rosen, as well as some literature he researched online and printed off that covered Christianity, prophecies, tribulation, armageddon, the rapture, and Revelation. "Thanks for the reading material. I'll certainly read it as quickly as I can digest it "Scott replied.

After Kelly left, Scott combined his reading material with a copy of the Holy Bible Contemporary English version that was given to him by Paige's granddaughter Jennifer, age twelve at the time, when she learned that her grandmother was going to marry Scott. Jennifer also enclosed the following letter:

Dear Scott, God said "Let there be light." On the first day he made the earth. This Bible is a gift from me to you. In the Bible you should look up John 3:16. It says "God loved us so much that he gave his only Son, so everyone who had faith in him will have eternal life and not really die." Read more to learn more about Jesus. Jesus did die on the cross for our sins and three days later he rose from the grave and ascended into heaven. He could have gotten off of the cross, but instead he chose to die so we wouldn't burn in hell. There is a heaven and a hell. Ask yourself this question, "Where would I go if I died right now?"You would go somewhere because you have a soul given to you by God. There is a devil who wants to trap and destroy everyone's life, including yours. He belongs in hell. All of the people who don't believe in Jesus will burn and that is why I'm here to help you. You're a good man and you deserve a chance. Everyone deserves a chance.

You are going to be my grandpa one of these days and I want you to go to heaven with us. Heaven is worth it all. In the Bible it talks about all of the streets paved with gold. That will be nice won't it? You also get all the food you want but the best that you would like is a mansion to live in. My favorite part is that I get to walk with Jesus in the park and we don't have to worry about any sickness or pain anymore.

In the Bible, it talks about all the good things that Jesus did. You probably already know that but, you didn't get to hear the whole story about the great things that Jesus did for us. To help, ask Jesus right now, "Please Jesus forgive me of all of my sins. Jesus please come into my heart, I know that I have done many bad things in the past, but now I am going to make a difference. I now believe that you're the one who died on the cross for my sins. Please come into my heart." For once, Scott this is the most important thing that I really want you to trust me on. Because, this is something you don't want to miss. You can do all things through Jesus Christ. I love Jesus so much. He's more than a friend to me, and more than a brother to me and he could be for you too.

I don't know if grandma told you but, of course you know Clayton(a cousin that almost drowned), I couldn't handle it anymore so I gave it to God and Jesus. I babysitted my mom's friend's kids and made $25. That Sunday I went to church and gave all of my money to God and told him, "I gave you my all, now give me your all back." Now Clayton is getting better and better. But, when you pray, don't expect it to always be done right then. You should PUSH. PUSH means, Pray Until Something Happens. If you give to God He will give you it all back He'll take care of you. Jesus will be all around you if you let him. If you fall, he will catch you. If you can't walk, he'll carry you. That's how awesome Jesus and God are.

Please take me seriously. Scott, I wouldn't tell you this if it wasn't true. I love you. With love, Jennifer.

* * *

Along with all of the other literature, Paige purchased A book named. Learn the Bible in Twenty-four Hours by Dr. Chuck Missler. "Wow you've certainly got your work handed to you, Scott. That's an enormous amount of reading material, When are you going to start this?" asked Paige. "I've been thinking about that and I don't think it's fair for me to read about Christianity before I understand Judaism. I don't really understand my own religion completely." "How are you going to do that?' Paige asked. "I don't even have a Jewish Bible. I need to get myself an English version of the Jewish Bible and I seriously doubt that the local bookstore has a copy. I'm going to check Amazon.com."

When Scott looked online, he found a book entitled <u>Complete Jewish Bible</u> (translation by David H. Stern, copyrighted 1998). He yelled for Paige "Come here and look at this. It's perfect. This is an English version of the Jewish Bible. I'm going to order it now."

When the book arrived, he excitedly began to read it. "I don't understand this. This book talks about both the Old and New Testaments. As far as I know there is only suppose to be the Old Testament. I don't understand what they are talking about old and new. In the new they're talking about the good news of Yeshua the Messiah and according to this, Yeshua is the Hebrew name for Jesus and in the New Testament it talks about Matthew, Mark, Luke and John. They also talk about Revelation. I don't understand!! Paige, this is Christianity, not Judaism."

Upon further, very close examination of his new Bible, Scott discovered that this was a Messianic Jewish Bible for Jews who honor Yeshua as their Messiah as well as Christians open to experiencing the Jewishness of their faith.

* * *

The stage was now set for what was yet to come.

Chapter XIII

DURING BREAKFAST THE next morning, Scott appeared to be in deep thought. Paige, looking up from her coffee, said, "Is anything wrong? You've been so quiet this morning." "I'm thinking about the <u>Complete Jewish Bible.</u> I've never heard of Messianic Judaism. I was raised only twenty or thirty miles from Time Square and there's a large population of Jewish people living in New York and I've never heard of Messianic Jews. I'd like to find a Messianic Jewish Synagogue near here and visit it." "That's a good idea," said Paige.

* * *

They went online and found a Messianic Jewish Synagogue located in Memphis, Tennessee. Scott called them and he was told the street address along with the times of service. "Paige, they have services every Saturday morning and they welcome anyone to attend."

* * *

Two weeks later after making arrangements for someone to babysit Risky, they drove to Memphis on Friday for the week-end, returning home on Sunday.

When they arrived for the service at B'RIT HADASHA Messianic Jewish Synagogue, they were warmly welcomed and Scott learned, just before the service began, that B'RIT HADASHA was the Hebrew translation meaning 'New Covenant.'

He looked around the congregation during the service and noticed that some of the men wore a *yamika* (skull cap), and some did not.

Some wore a *tallit* (prayer shawl), and some didn't. Part of the service was in English and part in Hebrew.

They read from the *Torah*, which is the first five Books of the Bible constituting the Pentateuch, the five books of Moses, (Genesis, Exodus, Leviticus, Numbers and Deuteronomy).

They sang songs in both Hebrew and English, which Paige recognized from hearing them at her own church. The women danced to Hebrew music and there was no doubt that they are a congregational home for both Jewish and Non Jewish believers that worship and serve the God of Abraham, Isaac and Jacob and to proclaim Yeshua (Jesus of Nazareth) as the Messiah of Israel and the whole earth.

* * *

On the drive home to Russellville, Scott said, I don't know about you, but I found this Synagogue to be very interesting. I'd like to go back and attend another service in the near future. How do you feel about it?" "I liked it very much. During the praise and worship, I felt like I was at home in my church."

Several weeks later, they returned to B'RIT HADASHA and during the visit Scott was approached by an elderly lady, with a Jewish accent, who said to him, "Do you know our Lord?" "No, he smiled.

* * *

The second visit had ignited his curiosity even more and after the service had concluded, Scott said, "I find this place intriguing and I would like to attend more, but the round trip drive is a killer not to mention the cost to do this very often."

Chapter XIV

A FEW DAYS after their trip to Memphis, Scott began to wonder just how many Messianic Jews there were in the world.

* * *

According to the Complete Jewish Bible, there are between 100,000 and 500,000 Messianic Jews in the English speaking countries and possibly twice as many in the world. The figures are very uncertain because it depends on whom one counts as Jewish and whom one counts as Messianic. It's obvious that most of the world's 13 to 17 million Jewish people do not accept Yeshua as the Messiah.

Online website Beth Adonai states there are estimated 175,000 Messianic Jews in the United States and one million worldwide.

According to Wikipedia, an online website, Messianic Judaism is a syncretic religious movement that arose in the 1960s and 1970s. It blends evangelical Christian theology with elements of Jewish practice and terminology.

Messianic Judaism usually holds that Jesus is both the Jewish Messiah "God the Son (one person of the Trinity), though some within the movement do hold to Trinitarian beliefs.

With few exceptions both the *Tanakh* (Old Testament) and the New Testament are believed to be authoritative and the divinely inspired Scripture.

Salvation, in most forms of Messianic Judaism, is achieved only through acceptance of Jesus as one's Savior. It is believed that all sin has been atoned for by Jesus' death and resurrection.

Jewish laws or customs that are followed are cultural and do not contribute to attaining salvation. Belief in the Messiah-ship and divinity of Jesus, which Messianic Judaism commonly shares, is viewed by many Christian denominations and Jewish religious movements as the defining distinction between Christianity and Judaism. Accordingly, Mainstream Christian groups usually accept Messianic Judaism as a form of Christianity.

Some adherents of Messianic Judaism are ethnically Jewish and many of them argue that the movement is a sect of Judaism. Jewish organizations and the Supreme Court of Israel (regarding the Law of Return), have rejected this claim and instead consider Messianic Judaism to be a form of Christianity.

From 2003 to 2007 the movement grew from 150 Messianic houses of worship in the United States to as many as 438, with over 100 in Israel and more world wide; congregations are often affiliated with larger Messianic Organizations or Alliances. In 2008, the movement was recorded to have between 6000 and 15,000 members in Israel and 250,000 in the U.S.

According to online website <u>Yahoo Answers</u>, How many Messianic Jews are there in the world? A Messianic Jew is a Jewish person who believes that Jesus (Yeshua) fulfilled the prophecies about the Messiah in the Jewish scriptures and He died to atone for the sins of mankind and that God raised Him from the dead on the third day

A Messianic Jew essentially is a Jewish person who believes that Jesus (Yeshua) is the promised Jewish Messiah. Also, the Messianic Jewish Alliance of America (MJAA) represents the interest of 100,000 Messianic Jews in the United States.

The MJAA is also affiliated with fifteen other National Messianic Alliances through an International Messianic Alliance which represents the interest of up to 350,000 Messianic Jews worldwide (figures are estimated by the Jewish Telegraph Agency 4/14/89).

* * *

Scott leaned back in his computer chair and said, "Wow, there's so much here to digest, but one thing is for certain; if I ever consider converting from mainstream Judaism to Messianic Judaism, I would be even more in a minority than I am now. Not only would anti Semitic Gentiles hate me, but even mainstream Jews would also find my Messianic views very offensive."

Chapter XV

For the next couple of weeks, Scott hardly looked at any of the religious material that he had collected. It seemed that whenever he attempted to read any of it he became irritable and distant as if some huge weight or force or even feelings of guilt distracted him. Paige noticed this and decided not to question him as her sixth sense advised her to allow him his privacy.

* * *

Paige was very pleased when Scott decided to accompany her to her church for Sunday services. After the service was over, as usual the family gathered in front of the church to make a decision concerning where to go for lunch. Scott winced when he noticed that his "old friend" Timothy Johnson and his wife were among the decision makers.

When Scott started the car and pulled out in back of the family caravan, on their way to the restaurant agreed upon, he said, "Is Timothy joining us for lunch?" "Looks that way," replied Paige. His knuckles turned white as he gripped the steering wheel and said, "Well I hope he doesn't attempt to 'Jew down' the waitress when the check arrives." "Now, be nice. I'm sure someone told him how you feel about that expression."

After waiting approximately forty-five minutes to be seated, Paige became nervous as Scott always turned into a 'semi monster' whenever he became extremely hungry.

* * *

Finally their food arrived and Scott's blood pressure returned to normal. During lunch the conversation turned to religion as it sometimes did after a Sunday service. He did not engage in the conversation, but only listened as he continued to eat. But, his attention picked up when the subject of heaven was mentioned. "All people must go thru Jesus to get to heaven," said Timothy. "You mean to say that everybody on the earth has to go thru Jesus to get to heaven?" asked Scott "That's right; everyone." "What about nice Jewish people or someone who has never heard of Jesus that did good deeds; they won't go to heaven?" Scott replied, raising his voice. "No, they won't. The Bible says that you must go thru Jesus to get to heaven," continued Timothy. "You mean to tell me that tribes in, in . . . the, I don't know, the Amazon Jungle some place like you would see on the National Geographic Channel, who have never heard of Jesus or Christianity, will not go to heaven if they live their life in a decent way?" "No, that's why we have missionaries." Scott continued, in an even louder voice, "I'm sure that there are places in absolutely no where that missionaries have never been and do you mean to tell me that they won't go to heaven?" Paige and her family became very nervous as this conversation continued. "Like I said before, they won't go to heaven." "I don't care what you say; there's nobody in this world that can say to me that my mother and father, who have passed away and were the kindest people you could know, are not in heaven right now." "Well, the Bible says." "I don't care what the Bible says; don't you say that my parents are not in heaven!!!!"Scott banged the table with his fist and yelled, "Timothy, do you mean to tell me that none of the Jewish people who perished in the Holocaust will go to heaven? It sounds like if all people feel the way you do, Hitler will have his final victory posthumously." Paige, feeling that Scott was about to turn over the table, reached for his hand and squeezed it. One of her children immediately changed the subject.

* * *

On the way home from the restaurant, Scott said to Paige, "There must be a plan that we do not know about or even understand that God makes for people like my parents. Whether you call him Jesus or Yeshua, there's no way that I could ever accept Messianic Judaism or Christianity if there's not a provision for those like my parents."

Chapter XVI

THE FOLLOWING DAY Greg visited Scott at home. He told him about the book of Revelation talking about the 144,000 Jews coming out of the tribulation and where to find this scripture. He wanted to also comfort Scott concerning who was and wasn't going to heaven, as Timothy had gone about this subject in a negative way. "Scott, I want you to know that I feel that your parents are in heaven."

* * *

After Greg's visit, Scott looked in Revelation of the <u>Complete Jewish Bible</u> which was titled the REVELATION of Yeshua the Messiah to Yochanan (Hebrew for John). Scott's understanding was that this was a revelation which God gave to Yeshua, the Messiah, of what must happen very soon, and He sent this prophecy by His angel to John.

In Revelation Chapter seven, it talked about John seeing four angels standing at the four corners of the earth, holding back the four winds of the earth, so that no wind would blow on the land, on the sea or on any tree. He saw another angel coming from the east with a seal from the living God, and He shouted to the four angels who had been given power to harm the land and the sea, "Do not harm the land or the sea or the trees until we have sealed the servants of our God on their foreheads!" John heard that there were 144,000 from every tribe of the people of Israel; twelve tribes, twelve thousand each were sealed.

In Revelation Chapter 14, John looked and saw the Lamb (Yeshua) standing on Mt. Tziyon; and with Him were 144,000 who had His name and His Father's name written on their foreheads. John then heard a sound from heaven which sounded like harpist playing on their harps and they were singing a new song before the throne and no one could learn this song except the 144,000 who had been ransomed from the world. They follow the Lamb and they have been ransomed from humanity as first fruits for God and the Lamb.

Scott turned to Paige, "Seems that Revelation is the last chapter of the New Testament, also called New Covenant of the Bible, which John saw in a vision and describes the end of the world and the 144,000 Jews who would be saved. Yeshua will be coming back and that all who had denied Him will know that He is the Messiah. There is so much in this chapter for me to understand at this time. I believe I would have to read this over and over again and discuss it with a Bible scholar, Rabbi or Pastor."

Chapter XVII

Scott delved more and more into his religious literature, including the Bible. The more Messianic Judaism made sense to him the more guilty he felt. He thought, "If I convert to Messianic Judaism, what would my parents think; especially my mother? I believe it would break her heart if she knew. I know that they have passed away and If they're in heaven, and I know they are, they know what I am doing here on earth. They would be upset with me. What would my sister say? When it comes to Judaism she seems to have taken the place of my mom. She goes to the Synagogue on high holy days. She makes Passover *seders*. I really don't want to hurt her."

* * *

The decision of converting from mainstream Judaism to Messianic Judaism was causing Scott a great amount of anguish. He felt that if he was wrong, it would be blasphemy. In the past he was quite a risk taker, but, in this case, he wouldn't be risking money. He would be risking his soul.

When he verbalized his feelings to Paige, she said, "Scott, I understand that you are concerned about what everyone would think about your decision, but we are responsible for our own lives and our own souls."

Chapter XVIII

IT WAS EARLY on a Sunday morning, in November 2004. Scott and Paige had not yet awakened. The dawn brought tragic news. They received a phone call from Greg notifying them that his daughter and their granddaughter Carisa Lynn Ennis, age twenty-six, had died in a horrible automobile accident. As choked up as Paige was, she managed to say to Greg, "Pray and trust in Jesus. She is with him now. Greg, pray for Jesus to give you strength." After the phone call she broke down and wept. Scott did his best to console her.

When Greg and Debbie arrived at Paige and Scott's home, Scott tried to console them and keep his cool, but lost control and cried.

The entire family gathered for the funeral and during the church service preceding the internment, Greg made a speech honoring his daughter and Scott thought how brave and strong he was to be able to accomplish this during this sad occasion.

During the visitation at the funeral home and even at the graveside, the family, pastor and Carisa's friends kept talking about how she was now with Jesus in heaven and was happy because heaven is a happy place. This triggered Scott's early memories when he was between six and seven, when he asked his mother about death. She told him that everyone dies. "Even me?" he questioned her. "Yes, everyone will die someday. But, don't you worry about that. It's a long way off." Then she tried to change the subject.

He did not hear anything about Jesus or heaven or that you would be in a nice place after you died. It bothered him that he would die someday and for some reason his young mind came up with the idea that a hundred years was a nice round number to live and that seemed far away. He remembered walking home from the Park Hill Theatre in

Yonkers after seeing a scene of someone dying. He recalled the name of the movie "Dark Victory" starring Bette Davis, where a young woman dies from a disease and the scene, through her eyes, as she is dying slowly fades to black. He was terrified. She was a young woman, definitely not a hundred years old.

As he walked home he tried to push the scene out of his mind and thought, "I'm seven years old now. I have ninety three more years to go and that's a long time." There was never any thought of heaven or even hell. His mom was a good mother and although she didn't mention the concept of heaven to him, she sent him to Hebrew school to get his Jewish education. Unfortunately everything was in Hebrew and all he learned was how to play hooky.

That fear of death has stayed with him all of his life and now that he is in his seventies, he feels that he is much closer to the end rather then the beginning and he wished that he could have that kind of faith Carisa's family had to comfort him.

Chapter XIX

LIFE IS FULL of sad and happy moments and just when Scott needed a happy moment after the death of Carisa, he received two e-mails; one from his daughter Tommy and also one from his daughter Maria.

Tommy was nine and Maria was eleven when his marriage had ended with their mother. Now they were eighteen and twenty. Maria had found Danny, Scott's son, on facebook and he gave her Scott's e-mail address.

He read Tommy's e-mail and she said that both she and Maria had missed him terribly. They wanted to be part of his life and wanted him to be part of theirs as well. The tears streamed down his face when he read the line that they missed him and loved him so much and wanted to hear from him as soon as possible. He almost lost it completely.

He sighed deeply as he opened Maria's e-mail. His joy was complete when she told him that she did not know how to start to tell him how much she missed him and she wanted to be in his life as well as he in hers.

Scott always believed, that after the divorce, he would never hear from the girls again, even though Paige told him several times that they would come back into his life. He received these two e-mails during the morning and throughout the day he told Paige about the happy moments he had experienced with his daughters before the divorce.

* * *

That evening, Katie and Jeff came over to visit and Scott couldn't wait to tell them the happy news of his daughters coming back into his life. As he tried to tell them his good news, Risky distracted him by pulling off one of Katie's shoes and making her go after him to retrieve it. He placed Risky in the kitchen and blocked him with a baby gate which separated him from everyone in the living room. In order to regain the family's attention, he put his front paws on the kitchen counter and stole one of the dish towels, prancing around so that Paige would become angry and take it away from him. He was a firm believer that bad attention was better than no attention. Scott said, "Hold on, Paige. The best thing you can do is ignore him. If you ignore him, he will calm down and occupy himself with something else." Risky looked at his 'daddy' with the dish towel dangling from his mouth and with a look that Scott thought meant "that's not fair."Everyone laughed and Scott retold for the hundred and fifty fifth time about his happy e-mails.

Tommy in U.S. Army

Maria

Chapter XX

SCOTT AND PAIGE decided to take a ride through Russellville. They had no particular direction in mind. They just drove aimlessly down this street and up that avenue. They were chatting with each other and enjoying the day.

As their car propelled them down Arkansas Avenue they noticed a sign adjacent to a building which basically said explore your Jewish roots with the days and times of services. When passing the sign Scott said, "Paige, did you see that? What is that?" "I don't know. I have never noticed that before." "I'm going to turn around and have a better look at that sign."

Scott made a u-turn and parked close so that he was able to see the sign more clearly. He saw a man on a ladder doing something with the sign. He also saw a phone number. He used his cell phone to call that number and the man working on the ladder answered his cell phone at the same time. Scott said, "We were passing by and saw your sign. What is this place all about?" The man replied, "Why don't you come in and visit with me and I will tell you all about it. Where are you now?" "Is that you on the ladder?" "Yes." "I can be there in a few seconds." "Great," he replied.

They pulled into the parking lot just as the man climbed down from the ladder and said, "Hi, I'm Randy Cook. Come on inside." He ushered them into a small chapel with no one else in attendance and the three of them sat down. "I'm Stanley Cohen and this is my wife, Paige." All three smiled and shook hands.

* * *

THE GREATEST RISK OF ALL

Randy explained to them that the place of worship was a Messianic Synagogue named Chiam B'Derech (Hebrew for Life in the Way) that recently moved into this building. He seemed particularly interested in Scott's last name "Cohen" (which in the Jewish religion means 'Priest'). Scott explained to him that he was raised Jewish and was now interested in learning about Messianic Judaism.

Randy invited then to attend *Shabbat* (the Jewish Sabbath from Friday night sundown to Saturday night sundown), which is held on Saturday mornings. "Thanks, for the information, Randy. Paige and I want to attend in the near future."

* * *

A few weeks later on a Saturday morning they attended the *Shabbat* service at Chiam B'Derech Messianic Synagogue. As they entered into this house of worship, Scott retrieved a *yamaka* from his pocket and placed it on his head. He was welcomed by Randy Cook, who took Scott aside and asked him, if he would recite the prayer which is usually reserved for "Cohens", if there is one available. "Randy it's been a very long time since I read Hebrew." "Don't worry, I'll help you through it," replied Randy. Scott reluctantly agreed as he knew his Hebrew was rusty at best.

* * *

Most of the men in the congregation wore *yamakas* and *tallits*. Randy 's wife, Beth approached Scott and offered to loan him a *tallit* but Scott said "No, thanks."

During the service he felt guilty that he refused to borrow the *tallit*, but he felt awkward because he knew that there was a prayer to be said before putting it on, which he did not remember and also that he was not sure which side went where.

He noticed that the service was mostly in Hebrew and once again he was faced with the problem of knowing when to stand and when to sit.

As the service was concluding, Randy announced in English. "This morning we have a very special guest with us. His name is Mr. Cohen and he is a real 'Cohen'. He is formally from New York and was raised Jewish. He is going to honor us by blessing the congregation."

Scott's heart raced as he slowly walked up in front of the congregation. As he read from the prayer, Randy stood next to him and whispered the correct pronunciation. When the prayer was completed, he sat down next to Paige, who smiled at him.

After the service, several of the congregation came to him and thanked him for his blessing. Scott beamed as he genuinely felt honored. The very friendly congregation, coupled with the graciousness of their leaders, Randy and Beth Cook, made for a warm and interesting experience.

* * *

Scott could not believe that a Messianic Jewish Synagogue was now in Russellville. He later looked online at the website of Chiam B'Derech, Life in the Way:

"We welcome and embrace all those who wish to learn more about the Hebrew roots of Christianity. We encourage you to join in learning to worship our Savior (Yeshua) in the manner in which he is most likely worshiped. We hope you explore with us while we focus on the way of life portrayed in the Holy Scriptures as we began to understand Him better in the context of the Jewish Rabbi that He personified. While there may be some who have Jewish lineage in our congregation, most of us are Gentiles as far as can be known. We believe God makes no distinction, but bestows His blessings on all who call upon Him and accepts His Son, Yeshua as the Messiah."

* * *

Scott planned to return to this place of worship, but somehow it reminded him of the times he attended the Congregation Sons of Israel Synagogue as a child and could not shake off those feelings of inadequacy when one is not knowledgeable enough to fit in.

Chapter XXI

SCOTT TOOK A special interest in all of Paige's grandchildren, and over time, he began to feel an almost blood chemistry with them. Her grandson, Matt, brought his girlfriend over to meet them and introduced Scott as his grandfather.

Both Matt and she were in their teens and the way that they looked at each other, it was obvious that this was a strong case of puppy love.

Their romance came to an abrupt end when her parents did not like Matt and influenced her to break off with him. When Matt told Scott and Paige about his dilemma, he had tears in his eyes. Scott advised him to call her father and try to find out the reason for their objection to him. He nervously dialed the phone and spoke to her father in a quiet respectful tone. Scott could hear her father screaming at Matt that he wanted him to stay away from his daughter and Matt could not get a word in edgewise. Scott grabbed the phone from Matt in order to reason with his 'never to be father-in-law'. He was rudely interrupted with "stay out of this Jew boy." With that Scott lost his cool. "You prejudice redneck. I'm a lot older than you, but on my worst day I could ring your neck," and he hung up the phone. His rage was not over. He began to kick a chair, slam his fist down on the breakfast bar and finally picked up a chair and flung it away from him, conveniently missing the television. Paige's son, Doug, witnessed this and said that Scott had selective aggression by not destroying the television set. When Doug said this, it caused Scott to laugh and lessoned his horrible moment. But, he was fed up with all the anti-Semitic remarks, as years and years of verbal abuse had caused him to reach his boiling point.

Scott continued his interest in Matt, watching him slowly mature. When Matt reached a crossroad in his life and did not know what direction to take next, Scott took him to the United States Navy recruiter. Matt made a high score on their entrance examination, but he decided not to join. He later attended college and got married, presenting Paige with two new great grandsons, namely Lucas and Ryan.

Matt did an imitation which always made everyone in his presence laugh. He would get on the floor with Risky, whom he pretended was a large crocodile, and in his best Australian accent, would imitate Steve Irwin saying, "Look at this big croc. Look at those teeth. You can see she's pregnant." Of course, Risky loved to be part of his act.

Chapter XXII

SCOTT CONTINUED TO read his religious material, but felt that he also needed another project in his life. He often told Paige about his first car, which he had when he was sixteen years old. It was a 1953 green four door customline Ford, V-8 with a three speed on the column standard shift. It was equipped with a radio, heater and turn signals.

He decided to go on the internet and type into the search engine, 1953 Ford. Not only did he find reference to this car, but several sites that sold antique cars. He spent endless hours researching antique cars from 1949-1957, especially fords.

Carrie bought him a book entitled <u>Cars of the Fabulous 50's</u>, A decade of high style and good times by James M. Flammang and the auto editors of Consumer Guide, (copyright 2001). He used this book as a reference while investigating these cars. He called numerous ads on cars that interested him, looking for exactly the right price, brand and model.

This search lasted about a year before he found a 1952 Ford, 2-door customline, with radio, heater, turn signals, outside sun-visor, V-8, 3 speed on the column and painted 'plum crazy'. This car had been restored, including a new interior of the times. There was little noticeable change in the body styles of 1952-53 Fords. Then he waited patiently for his car to be shipped from Pennsylvania to Russellville.

He was very friendly with his neighbor, Jerry Smith, who was a mechanic in his own right and with his help the car was converted from a 6-volt to a 12-volt. The engine and trunk were detailed and an am/fm/cd player with 4 speakers, seatbelts, rebuilt carburetor and various missing trim were installed.

Since Arkansas is very hot in the summer, he had a local antique car specialist install an in-dash air conditioner, which he had purchased from a company specializing in air conditioning for antique cars.

Scott and Paige rode around Russellville in their new "bomb" with fuzzy dice hanging from the rear view mirror. One day they ran out of gas, when returning from a restaurant in Paris, Arkansas. It was then that he learned that his car was empty when the gauge registered ¼ full. He made a quick call to Jerry who brought them the necessary gas to continue on their journey.

He was in seventh heaven. He was now sixteen again and Paige was 15, although she refused to wear bobby socks.

Chapter XXIII

SCOTT WAS VERY excited when he received his son Danny's phone call announcing that he would be getting married and the wedding was scheduled to be in Ireland. "What part of Ireland?" "Bangor, Pop. It's about twenty miles from Belfast," Danny replied. "Belfast? Isn't that the place where they had all the problems with Catholics and Protestants fighting each other?" "That's right, Dad but that is all over now."

When Scott and Paige went online to book a flight to Ireland, they learned that the lowest cost airfare would be to connect in New York City and fly to Dublin. He thought it would be a great idea to lay over in New York for a couple of days in order to show Paige where he grew up in Yonkers, New York. They stayed in a motel in Yonkers the night they arrived and the next morning they began their tour.

He drove to South Yonkers and showed Paige the apartment house on Radford Street. It was a fourth floor walk up (with no elevator) small two bedroom, one bath apartment, where he lived with his parents and sister from the age of five to fourteen. He did not include, in the tour, where his parents lived (Nichols Ave, Yonkers, NY) when he was born, because they had moved from that address shortly afterwards and lived throughout the mid-west as his father did plumbing work on army barracks at various forts. They then moved back to Yonkers in order for Scott to begin kindergarten when he turned five.

He then drove the short distance to the synagogue on Elliott Avenue at the Congregation Sons of Israel, where he received his religious education. He stopped in front of this house of worship and again the memories of his feelings of inadequacy; whereby he did not know when to sit, when to stand and did not understand The Hebrew prayers, came back to haunt him. He thought about going in and showing Paige the inside of the synagogue, but had no way of knowing if he could get in and it was raining, he rationalized to himself.

From there they drove a few blocks to Broadway to see the Park Hill Movie Theatre where he had spent many Saturday afternoons. The theatre appeared to be permanently closed, but he was happy to see that its marquee was still in place.

He then drove to PS 27 (public school) where he had attended kindergarten, which was now a Montessori school. He turned to Paige and said, "I definitely would not fit in there now." He laughed. They then went to PS 3 where he had attended grade school 1-6. This school was permanently closed.

From there he drove to North Yonkers where he lived in a nicer two-bedroom apartment with his parents from age 14-16 and then on to Gorton High School where he attended his freshman to sophomore year. He then drove to Roosevelt High School where he completed his Junior and Senior years.

Scott drove to the Colonial Heights section where he visited the first house, built by his father, for his mother on Cliffside Drive and finally to the second house built by his father for his family in Mohican Heights on Iroquois Road. When he parked in front of the stone wall surrounding the house, the memories of his '53 ford in the driveway and the countless hours he and his friends sat on the wall talking about their girlfriends along with their dreams and aspirations clearly resurfaced.

He wanted to take Paige to the universities in New York City he had attended. He wondered if his fraternity house on Sullivan Street a few blocks from "Little Italy" was still there. Unfortunately, time was short and part of the tour could not be completed.

The next day, they caught a plane to Ireland and landed the next morning (middle of the night on their body clock).

Paige was amused when they rented a car for their trip from Dublin to Belfast and saw Scott sitting behind the steering wheel on the wrong side of the car and shifting the 5-speed manual transmission with his left hand. He had driven before on the "English" side of the road, as he had lived and worked in Hong Kong and on the Island of St. Kitts, but after driving a few miles of the approximately one hundred mile two hour trip, he realized that he was a lot younger then when he drove on the "wrong" side of the road and this trip turned out to be treacherous. They both breathed a sigh of relief when they pulled into their hotel in Belfast.

* * *

The wedding, which was in Bangor, was a beautiful affair and the ceremony was a combination of Christian and Jewish, including the breaking of the glass.

During the reception, Scott lifted his glass and toasted his son Danny and his lovely bride, Nichola.

Chapter XXIV

EVER SINCE SCOTT had moved to Russellville, he felt that he was living in Paige's house. He had mentioned this to her numerous times and they both agreed that, in order for them both to be completely happy, they needed to move to another house. Scott loved projects and he enjoyed driving, with Paige and Risky, around Russellville looking for their dream house.

It was summertime and the temperature had exceeded 100 degrees. Whenever they went into a house, they left Risky in the car with the air conditioner running and the window cracked. He always waited patiently.

The search was a long process until they found just the perfect house for them. They sold Paige's house, closed on their new house, and with the help of her granddaughter, Kellie DeAnn, the packing was completed.

As they were getting ready to move into the new house, Paige began to experience an overwhelming feeling of trepidation. Risky was now a little over two years old and still in his puppyhood. Previously in the old house, he had eaten part of the carpet, chewed up their deck, bit off a piece of their grandfather clock, chewed the control handle of the recliner and one day, because they left him alone, he was either bored or angry, he retaliated by chewing a hole in the wall of the hallway.

The hallway had to be plastered and re-wallpapered. Paige was petrified that he would ruin her new house. Also, the backyard had new sod which had not had time to knit together and this resulted in a very muddy backyard. She shared her fears with Scott who tried, in vain, to quiet her fears.

Scott loved Risky with all his heart and even though he had spent endless hours in oppressive heat, searching for the new house, he was now going to be banished to who knows where.

Paige made an agreement with Risky's groomer to find a good home with kids free of cost and that he would continue to be an inside dog. The groomer who knew the Cohens and Risky well felt sorry for the both of them and said he would find Risky a home, but the new owner's name would be sealed just like an adoption.

Risky spent one night in the new house and in the morning Scott, with Paige, reluctantly drove Risky to the groomer. When he got close to his destination, he broke down and cried. "It's alright, Scott. Let's just take Risky home and forget about doing this." "No, Paige. I love Risky, but I love you more and I know you have a terrible fear of Risky destroying the new house and you're going to be miserable."

When the groomer came to the car, he took Risky's leash and led him into the shop. For Scott, this was a very dark day.

Several days passed and Paige could see that Scott was very moody. He had little to say. Practically all of her children had dogs and Scott told Paige that he did not want any of their dogs in their house nor did he want to hear about them. Paige could not bear to see Scott in this awful state. She also loved Risky and missed him. She was genuinely worried about his well-being. She called the groomer in the hopes of retrieving him and learned that he was placed with a family. His new owner's name was confidential and supposedly had children. "Scott, Risky is with a new family that have children to play with and I'm sure he will be well taken care of." "How do you know?" he replied. Scott knew that he would never see Risky again because he was a beautiful Golden Retriever and his new family will get him for free and they would certainly keep him.

Days passed, Scott was still very sad. He was angry with himself for not putting his foot down and refusing to let Risky go. He had prayed to God on numerous occasions, but he never prayed directly to Jesus. He read a lot of the religious literature and learned of miracles that was said that Jesus performed and he felt what did he have to lose by asking Jesus to give him back Risky.

About five weeks had passed since Risky was given away. Paige along with her daughter and friend Annette were having dinner in Little Rock. Scott was at home when he heard the door bell ring. When he got to the door, he saw a van with the name of the grooming establishment, backing out of the driveway. He waved for the van to stop and the groomer pulled back into the driveway. The door opened and out came Risky, who looked bewildered. "What happened? How did you get Risky back?" asked Scott. "The people who took him, brought him back this morning and they do not want him anymore," he replied.

Scott noticed a sore spot on his nose which was not there before. "Is he alright?" "He seems to be. He was very dirty when I received him and he had burrs in his fur as if he has been an outside instead of an inside dog. I cleaned him very well and also trimmed his hair and cut his nails. I'm glad he's back with you." "I prayed to Jesus for Risky to come home," Scott said, realizing that this was the first time he had vocalized this. The groomer said, "Well, he's back now." "Thanks again," said a happy Scott.

Scott led Risky through the garage and into the house and removed his leash. He looked around like he did not remember the one night he had spent in this house. Scott fed and watered Risky from his old food and water bowls.

He called Paige and said "You're not going to believe who is here." "Who?" asked Paige. "Risky." "How did you get him back?" "I'll tell you when you get home."

Scott petted and talked to Risky as he waited for "Risky's mama" to arrive home. When the garage door opened, Risky ran to Paige with his huge tail wagging. He jumped up and licked her face. Risky was home to stay.

Chapter XXV

THE COHENS, INCLUDING Risky, were beginning to settle into their new home. This meant to Scott that he was no longer living in Paige's house. He was now living in their house.

* * *

Everyday, Scott walked down his sloped driveway to get his mail. Very subtly, he began to notice that it was becoming increasingly difficult to walk. In order to not lose his balance and fall, he started to walk down by zig-zagging back and forth in order to reduce the steepness of its slope. When he reached the street to retrieve his mail, he began walking back and forth to exercise. He would try to increase his distance every trip by walking a little further and measuring it by the mail boxes he passed.

One day while walking, he experienced a severe pain in his right upper thigh, very near his hip. He had to rest a short time before continuing on. After a while, he regained his composure and returned home, sitting in his easy chair to alleviate the pain.

Next morning, he had problems getting out of bed and felt a sharp pain in his lower back. He was confused as to what was happening to him, because the thigh pain had subsided and was now only in his back. He called his physician and was prescribed pain medicine for the back pain. The pain continued to be severe and Paige assisted him in walking from the bed to the bathroom.

In 1979, he had suffered a back injury. In 1989, he was diagnosed with Crohn's disease, which is a chronic inflammatory condition of the gastrointestinal tract, and, as a result had to have his small intestine re-sectioned. He also had a double hip replacement.

Now, due to the pain skipping around, he was unsure of where it was actually originating. To further complicate the issue, he was having problems with sleeping, even with sleep aids.

One night, as he lay in bed trying desperately to sleep and blocking out the pain, his fear of the unknown began to engulf him and even though his eyes were closed, and with the bedroom dark, he started to see a light in front of him.

What he saw was fuzzy in the beginning, but he could focus on what appeared to be a large hand, with its palm up, and cherubims circling in and out. Then, the hand and cherubims disappeared. He then saw an image of Jesus from the waist up, wearing a white robe with jet black hair falling over his shoulders. The light that surrounded Jesus was indescribably bright. It was brighter than anything he had ever seen. There was no sound and no communication.

His eyes opened abruptly and he said in a loud voice to Paige, "I saw a vision of Jesus. I don't think I was dreaming." He then began to cry. He explained exactly what he had seen and said it looked like a painting of Jesus that he had seen before. He continued to talk about the bright light. He said the intensity of the light was not earth-like and when he tried to recall the vision in his mind, he could recall everything except the intensity of the brightness of the light. He could not duplicate the light . . . . not even in his own imagination.

* * *

The next morning, Scott reasoned that the large hand with its palm up was Jesus' hand lifting him up from his misery. He also reasoned that his vision of Jesus, looking like a previous painting he had seen before, was because no one in modern times knows exactly how Jesus looks, and he was no exception as to knowing how Jesus should look. Scott believed that Jesus appeared in this manner to show him who he really was, unlike the dream he experienced before when Jesus appeared as just an ordinary man, not wearing a robe, but modern day clothes. This was different. He believed that he again, had seen Jesus.

Chapter XXVI

TIME PASSED AND Scott showed no improvement. One night, Paige finally found it necessary to call 911. When he arrived at the ER it was determined that in addition to his back pain and sleep deprivation, his Crohn's disease had exacerbated, resulting in the need for a blood transfusion. He was given morphine for his pain as well as a sedative to sleep.

When he awoke, several hours later, he was in a semi-private room and Paige was sitting by his bed smiling at him. She had become friendly with Diane Morris, the daughter-in-law of Fred Morris, a man in his nineties who was Scott's roommate.

Paige had learned that Fred was waiting for Hospice to make arrangements to move him into their care, but, they were delayed in their arrangements, which should have been completed before Scott was placed in the room with him. Also, Fred's son, Bob, was there with his wife Diane. She was very upset because Fred, who was close to dying, had not yet accepted Jesus as his Savior, into his heart. Fred had reasoned that no merciful God would send His Son to the cross to be crucified.

Diane described him as a real Arkansas mountain man, set in his ways and proud of his independent spirit.

Paige contacted her daughter-in-law Debbie, who called We Care Ministries of the First Assembly of God Church of Russellville, to not only pray for Scott's health, but to try and convince Fred to accept Jesus as his Savior and ask for forgiveness for his sins, in order for him to enter into the Kingdom of Heaven.

The church sent one of its representatives to St. Mary's Hospital to visit Scott and Fred. Upon arriving, he visited Scott, praying with him for his health to return. Then, he walked to Fred's side of the room and introduced himself to him and his family. He tried to reach Fred and convince him of his need for Jesus, but to no avail. He then returned to Scott's bedside.

Paige felt compelled to go to Fred's bedside; that God was urging her to do so. "Mr. Morris, my name is Paige Cohen. My husband is your roommate. He is in the next bed and I want to talk to you about Jesus. Do you know Jesus?" Fred nodded affirmatively. "Would you like Jesus to forgive you of your sins?' Again he nodded affirmatively. Paige began to recite the sinner's prayer stopping every few words allowing him to repeat after her. "Jesus." "Jesus," repeated Fred, "Please forgive my sins." Again Fred repeated, "Jesus, please forgive my sins." "And save my soul." "And save my soul," Fred concluded,

Diane began to weep, the representative from the church began to praise God and Scott started to cry as he realized, in that moment, that God had placed him in that room at that particular time, in order for him to be instrumental in convincing this wonderful elderly man to ask Jesus' forgiveness for his sins.

Later that day, Fred was transferred into Hospice's care. Scott was stabilized, released from the hospital the following day and given an appointment in Little Rock with a neurosurgeon to diagnose his back pain.

Fred passed away a short time later, but not before Diane baptized him.

Chapter XXVII

THE NEUROSURGEON DIAGNOSED Scott with spinal stenosis and a pronounced bulging disc. He was advised to undergo a series of steroid injections. He completed these, but the pain continued to return. He was also advised to undergo physical therapy for the pain and his increasing walking problem.

He began walking with a cane and later had to move to a walker. He went to two neurologists, one of which, administered nerve conductive tests. He was told that there was nothing more to be done. He would need to use pain medication, and exercise as much as possible. One doctor stated, "use it or lose it." He was finally told to accept using a walker and not feel self conscious about it.

* * *

On Scott's 70th birthday, he was surprised with a visit from his sons, David with his girlfriend, and Danny with his wife, Nichola. He was thrilled. This surprise was a well kept secret by Paige who helped them coordinate it. The visit was great and overall it was a wonderful week-end.

This visit took his mind off of his back and walking problems and during their visit, the family pet ambassador, Risky, licked their faces, stole their shoes and attempted to steal food from their plates.

* * *

After this was all over, Scott returned to his reading and attempting to digest his religious material.

Chapter XXVIII

SCOTT JUST DIGESTED a stack of pancakes that Paige had prepared for his breakfast. It was a beautiful morning and he decided to walk out onto his back deck. Risky followed him out, as usual. He sat down on the outdoor couch and waited for Risky to sit beside him. Just as Risky was about to reach Scott's side, he stopped and layed down, starting to tremble uncontrollably. He could move his front legs, but his hind legs appeared to be paralyzed.

Scott thought he was choking on something or having a problem with his breathing. He immediately rushed to his side. "Paige, come out here quickly. Risky is having trouble breathing." She dropped what she was doing and joined Scott. "Paige, I don't think he can breathe." They tried to open his mouth to see if anything was lodged inside, but could not manage to pry it open. Scott looked at Paige, in a helpless manner. She said, "Breathe, Risky. Jesus, please don't let him die." "Jesus, help him," joined in Scott.

Paige opened the back door to go in and call the veterinarian. Risky crawled with his front paws through the opened door, dragging his paralyzed backside and hind legs over to his blanket into the dining room where he slept. They joined him at his blanket and continued to pray and comfort him.

Risky, who was completely housebroken and had been for some time now, defecated and urinated. It was apparent that his paralysis had caused him to lose control of his bodily functions.

After what seemed to be an eternity, which was actually about three to four minutes, Risky returned to normal. When Paige reached the veterinarian and described what had happened, he told her that Risky had suffered a seizure. He said to keep him quiet for the remainder of the day and to log the date and time of the seizure. Blood tests were performed and the Cohens were advised that if he had no more than three or four seizures per year, he would be okay.

Almost one year to the date of the first seizure, Risky suffered approximately ten seizures in one day. They again prayed for him to be okay, but feared that this time he was going to die. Scott knelt beside Risky, "Jesus, please help him."

At that time he was prescribed phenobarbital (two pills twice daily) and valium to be given in case of multiple seizures. The medicine worked. His seizures reduced to one or two per year and he no longer had multiple episodes.

Risky seemed to know when he was getting ready to have a seizure and would always get as close to Paige as possible. She was his 'mama' who always comforted him and talked him through the seizure.

* * *

The time leading to Risky's birthday was marked by happy events. Scott's sister, Doris, from upstate New York, visited him. His daughter, Tommy, joined the Army Reserve and successfully completed her six months of active duty, before returning to college. It was hard for him to imagine that his little daughter, who was nine at the time of the divorce, had completed the Army basic training course.

Scott and Paige were also overjoyed when Danny and Nichola announced the birth of his grandson Samuel Logan Cohen.

When Risky's sixth birthday finally arrived, he presented his parents with a wonderful gift. His puppyhood had finally ended, and he was more calm and well-behaved, at least for Risky.

Danny, Nichola & Sam

Chapter XXIX

IT WAS A rainy night, Paige made some popcorn and she and Scott were watching television. They were watching a movie entitled "Stolen Summer." It was a 2002 movie which depicted a Rabbi's son, ten or eleven years old, who learned he was dying. His young friend, an Irish Catholic boy, approximately twelve years old, comes up with a plan to ensure that his Jewish friend goes to heaven.

The young Catholic boy claimed that Jews cannot get into heaven. The movie did end on a good note as the young Catholic boy proclaimed, after the death of his friend, that indeed he was in heaven. He also stated that Jews as well as other non-Christians may go to heaven as long as they pray to their god and are righteous.

Somehow that Jews do not go to heaven struck a nerve in Scott as it reminded him of the saying 'the Jews killed Jesus;' a remark that he heard throughout his childhood and in to his adulthood. "Paige, I've heard all my life that the Jews killed Jesus, which means to me that they did not like him for what he was saying and he was plotted against and then killed." "How do you know that he wasn't liked and by whom?" asked Paige. "I have referenced the Complete Jewish Bible (translation by David H. Stern) and the Holy Bible New International Version and according to the Old Testament in Psalms 118: 22, it was prophesied, 'The very rock that the builders rejected has become the cornerstone'. To me this means that Jesus was rejected by the Jewish leadership and this prophecy was fulfilled in the New Covenant (New Testament) in Matthew21:42 Yeshua (Jesus) said to them, 'Haven't you ever read in the *Tanakh* (Old Testament), the rock which the builders rejected has become the cornerstone!' This had come from ADONAI (God), and in our eyes it is amazing?'

This was also fulfilled in the B'RIT HADASHAH (New Testament), in John 7:48. 'Have any of the authorities trusted him?' Or any of the P'rushim (Pharisees)? No!'

Paige, Jesus was plotted against by both Jew and Gentile together. Psalms 2:1-2 the New Covenant says, 'Why do the nations conspire and the peoples plot in vain? The kings of the earth take their stand and the rulers gather together against His Anointed One.'

This means to me that 'the nations' represent Gentiles, 'the people' represent the Jews and 'the Anointed One' refers to Jesus. This prophecy is fulfilled in the New Testament, Acts 4:27 which says, 'This has come true in this city, since Herod and Pontius Pilate with *goyim* (non Jews) and the people of Israel, all assembled against your Holy Servant Jesus, whom you made Messiah.'

I believe Acts 4:27 speaks for itself, and Acts 4:28 says, 'do what your power and plan had already determined beforehand should happen.' This is amazing stuff. According to this, that was God's plan that Jesus be plotted against by the Jews and Gentiles together. It was prophesied that Jesus be executed by crucifixion by having his hands and feet pierced. This was prophesied in the Old Testament, Psalms 22:16-17 saying 'Dogs have surrounded me; a band of evil men has encircled me, they have pierced my hands and feet. I can count all my bones; people stare and gloat over me.'

This is also prophesied in Zachariah 12:10 saying, 'And I will pour out on the house of David and the inhabitants of Jerusalem a spirit of grace and prayer. They will look on me, the one they have pierced, and they will mourn for him as one mourns for an only child, and grieve bitterly for him as one grieves for a first born son.' Paige, this is obvious to me, that it is prophesied that Jesus would be executed by crucifixion, by having his hands and feet pierced.'

Matthew 27:35 says, 'After they had nailed him to the cross, they divided his clothes among them by gambling.' This is further fulfilled in Luke 24:39 which says, 'Look at my hands and my feet. It is I myself! Touch me and see; a ghost does not have flesh and bones.' This is also fulfilled in John 19:18 saying 'Here they crucified Him by nailing Him to the execution stake (cross) along with two others—one on each side with Jesus in the middle.'

Paige, it is interesting to note in John 19:19 that Pilate had a notice written and placed on the cross. He put 'Yeshua from Nazareth, King

THE GREATEST RISK OF ALL

of the Jews.' This is obvious to me that Pilate directed the execution of Jesus and Pilate was definitely not Jewish. He also referred to Jesus as King of the Jews. This was an example of a non-Jew killing a Jew. It was further fulfilled in John 19:34-37, 'However, one of the soldiers stabbed his side with a spear, and at once blood and water flowed out.' I doubt that this soldier was Jewish. It goes on to say 'The man who saw had testified about it, and his testimony is true. And he knows that he tells the truth so you too can trust. For these things happened in order to fulfill this passage of the Old Testament 'not one of his bones will be broken.' And, again, they will look at Him Who they have pierced.'

Further to this John 20:20-28 states, 'After he said this, he showed them his hands and side. The disciples were overjoyed when they saw the Lord. Again Jesus said, 'Peace be with you!' As the Father has sent me,' I am sending you.' And with that he breathed on them and said 'Receive the Holy Spirit. If you 'Now Thomas (called Didymus), one of the Twelve, was not with the disciples when Jesus came. So the other disciples told him, 'We have seen the Lord!' But he said to them, 'Unless I see the nail marks in his hands and put my finger where the nails were, and put my hand into his side. I will not believe it.'

A week later his disciples were in the house again and Thomas was with them. Though the doors were locked, Jesus came and stood among them and said, 'Peace be with you!' Then he said to Thomas, "Put your finger here; see my hands. Reach out your hand and put it into my side. Stop doubting and believe.' Thomas said him, 'My Lord and my God.' Paige, I believe this is where the expression 'doubting Thomas' comes from.

Finally, in Revelation1:7 the Bible says: 'Look, he is coming with the clouds,' and every eye will see him, even those who pierced him; and all the peoples of the earth will mourn' because of him. 'So shall it be! Amen.'

Paige, do you realize that when people say the Jews killed Jesus, I believe that most of those who say this, don't even know that Jesus is the English name for Yeshua, which is His Hebrew name.

Yeshua was a Jew and still is. In fact, He was a Jewish Rabbi. He was rejected by the Jewish leadership (not all of the Jews) because they did not agree that He was the Messiah—their Messiah and they believed what he was teaching was blasphemy. In their hearts, they felt that they were right. He was plotted against by the Jewish leadership who strongly disagreed with him and conspired with the Gentiles (in this case Romans) under the command of Pontius Pilate.

But, putting this all aside, it was prophesied in the Old Testament and fulfilled in the New Testament that Jesus would be crucified, because the central message of the Bible, which is the Word of God, is telling about God, his people, and His Messiah. The Bible's constant theme is that human beings need to be saved, and that God provides salvation. In the days of old, in order to be forgiven for ones sins, animals were slaughtered. It was God's plan that Yeshua, who was sinless 'a lamb without blemish' would be God's Lamb . . . . taking away the sins of the world.

You know, it was **GOD'S PLAN** that Jesus, the Messiah, had to be killed. If Jesus was not executed and died a natural death then maybe we would still be sacrificing animals at the alter and there would be no Christianity. Christians come from the word Christ which evolved from the Greek word 'Christos' which means Messiah.

When Jesus claimed to be the Messiah, 'the Anointed One', some of the Jewish people believed in Him and followed him and still believed in him after he was crucified and rose. These Jews split from the mainstream Jews who did not believe Jesus is the Messiah and those were eventually called Christians and thus was born Christianity. As the centuries passed, and somewhere in time, Christians either forgot or denied their Jewish roots."

Scott took a deep breath and his voice raised a couple of octaves as he said, "If some Jewish Rabbi (known only to his peers) was killed today while conducting services in his Synagogue, in a small town somewhere, and one of his Jewish members took out a gun and shot him; and if this was on the evening news, I doubt that the rest of the world would remember that a Jewish Rabbi was killed by a fellow Jew a couple of months later.

But, unfortunately I believe that for some time to come there will be Gentiles who will keep saying that the Jews killed Jesus. Thank God for the educated people who understand that it was prophesied and the prophecy was fulfilled of how and why Yeshua is the 'Lamb of God.'"

* * *

Paige realized, at this time, that this subject of the Jews killing Jesus, was a festering sore for Scott, as he had been taunted with this, especially in his childhood.

Chapter XXX

SCOTT CONTINUED TO have a great deal of back pain and received more steroid injections. He was becoming very discouraged with his health.

His misery was pleasantly interrupted when his daughter Maria called and announced that she and her husband, Brian had just given him a new grandson named Andres Joel Medina Cohen.

* * *

Scott's joy was short lived as his symptoms worsened. His maladies were complicated, when Paige was diagnosed with spinal stenosis and she elected to receive back surgery. During her convalescent period she fell and broke her left wrist. Because she was feeling numbness in the lower portion of her body, an MRI was performed. It was discovered that she now had an infection in her back. This resulted in a second back surgery and in order to clear up the infection, she had to receive antibiotics at home, 24/7 by means of intravenous for six weeks.

While all of this was happening Scott, began to worsen and both of them were virtually incapacitated at the same time.

Paige's family rallied around them. Her daughters, Katie and Carrie took turns practically living with them to get them through this terrible time; at least until they where able to fend for themselves.

In addition, her grandchildren Matt, Jennifer, Tyler, Taylor, Hanna and Nick had to donate their time, in order to shore things up. Her sons Greg and Kelly, son-in-law Gregg as well as her daughters-in-law, Debbie and Margie made sure that their food shopping was completed and their prescription medicine was renewed. Also, Debbie arranged for the First Assembly of God We Care Ministry, to provide meals for Scott and Paige.

Paige started to improve at the same time Scott's condition seriously worsened. The doctors could not yet find the source of his affliction. He was losing weight and getting weaker.

On an Easter Sunday, he noticed a large protruding mass on his upper thigh. The next day he visited an orthopedic surgeon and was subsequently advised that it was an infection, which required a hip replacement of his right hip that was previously replaced in 1989.

During the surgery, it was discovered that the infection was more extensive than previously thought and had completely engulfed his right hip. After the new hip was replaced, he was placed on a regiment, at home, of powerful antibiotics fed intravenously for six weeks to eliminate this life threatening infection.

While receiving antibiotics at home, he relapsed and was rushed to the ER. It was there that they found that he had suffered kidney damage coupled with dehydration. In addition, he completely lost his appetite and had to be provided nourishment intravenously. The doctors were concerned that while he was receiving the antibiotics, they could not give him a drug called Remicade which was used to control his Crohn's disease since the year 2000.

During this time, he was visited and prayed for by Senior Pastor Ronnie Morris, Pastor Ben Andrews, Pastor Mike Norberg and Pastor Bud Avants.

Scott's weight had dropped to one-hundred and eight pounds. He felt as if he was going to die and he prayed to Yeshua to help him. He recited the sinner's prayer.

Little by little, his chemistry started to improve and he was finally released after nine days to complete his antibiotics at home. He was visited daily by Home Health Care and Physical Therapy. Eventually, he completed the antibiotic treatment. His infection disappeared, his appetite returned and he began to gain his weight back.

His back pain disappeared and when he returned to his gastroenterologist he was informed, by his doctor, that he thought that Scott's Crohn's disease had burned itself out and was now gone, even though there is no known cure for Crohn's disease. As far as Scott was concerned this was another miracle performed by Yeshua and also that his body alerted him of his impending doom on Easter Sunday.

Chapter XXXI

SCOTT WAS SO thankful and excited that the Lord had pulled him from the depths of despair and even though he still had to use a walker, he was definitely a new man, health-wise.

Scott had never considered himself a religious man however, Paige purchased a *menorah* (a nine-branched candelabrum) used on the Jewish holiday of Hanukkah (an eight day Jewish celebration, known as the Festival of Lights), which according to the Talmud, one of Judaism's most central text, Judah Mccabee and the other Jews who took part in the rededication of the Second Temple witnessed what they believed to be a miracle. Even though there was only enough untainted olive oil to keep the menorah's candles burning a single day, the flames continued flickering for eight nights, leaving them time to find a fresh supply.

His sister Doris would call him every year on the anniversary of the death of his parents (this date varied from year to year because it was based on the Jewish calendar), so that he could light a *Yahrzeit* candle (a candle that burns for twenty-four hours on the anniversary of a death) in their memory.

Now he was more eager to read and understand the Complete Jewish Bible. He was very intrigued by the prophecies and their fulfillment concerning Yeshua.

His favorite one, which caused him to be in awe, was found in Daniel 9:24-26 (Complete Jewish Bible) "Seventy weeks have been decreed for your people and for your holy city for putting an end to the transgression, for making an end of sin, for forgiving iniquity, for bringing in everlasting justice, for setting the seal on vision and prophet, and for anointing the Especially Holy Place, Know, therefore, and discern that seven weeks (of years) will elapse between the issuing of the decree to restore and rebuild *Yerushalayim* (Jerusalem) until an anointed prince comes.. It will remain built for sixty-two weeks (of years), with open spaces and moats; but these will be troubled times. Then after the sixty-two weeks, *Mashiach* (Messiah) will be cut off and have nothing. The people of a prince yet to come will destroy the city and the sanctuary, but his end will come with a flood and desolations are decreed until the war is over.

This prophecy was fulfilled as referenced in the Complete Jewish Bible in Romans 5:6 "while we were still helpless, at the right time, the Messiah died on behalf of ungodly people."

This was further fulfilled in I Peter 3:18 "For the Messiah himself died for sins, once and for all, a righteous person on behalf of unrighteous people, so that he might bring you to God. He was put to death in the flesh, but brought to life by the Spirit."

Scott referenced Daniel 9:24-26 in both his Bibles and the internet as follows:

The Hebrew word for "week" used in this passage is shavuah, which means "period of seven. From the context and the external evidence regarding the book of Daniel, the term means a unit of seven years, and that the prophecy deals with seventy times seven years, or 490 years. The word authorizing the rebuilding of Jerusalem probably refers to the edict of Artaxerxes, in about 445 B.C.E. Therefore, 490 years brings us to the first half of the first century of the Common Era. But during the nineteenth century, A British scholar, Sir Robert Anderson, sought to perform much more refined calculations in an effort to pinpoint the intended date. He, in his book the Coming Prince, explains that a year in Jewish calculations at the time of Daniel was 360 days.

According to Daniel,The Messiah will come 173,880 days after Artaxerxes' decree because the 69 weeks of verse 25 amount to 483 years, which can be multiplied by 360 days (483x360=173,880). This passage can be read as 'seven weeks and threescore and two weeks' rather than breaking it up as in the above translation.

The date Artaxerxes' decree was March 14, 445 B.C.E. because the first day of Nisan (Nehemiah 2:1-6) fell on March 14 in 445, according to the Royal Observatory in Greenwich, England. Anderson figures the imprecise "in the month of Nisan" to be the first day because the Mishnah (the first major work of Rabbinic Judaism written in Hebrew) explains that the first of Nisan "is a new year for the computation of the reign of Kings and for festivals."

Anderson sets the day for Jesus' entry to Jerusalem as April 6, 32 C.E. Luke said Jesus began His ministry in the fifteenth year of Tiberius Caesar, whose reign began in 14 C.E. Most scholars agree that Jesus' ministry continued for three years, which brings us to 32 C.E. John(12:1) says Jesus went to Bethany "six days before the Passover" and that He entered Jerusalem the "next day" (12:12). Passover is always 14 Nisan, which according the Royal Observatory, fell on Thursday, April 10, 32 C.E. Thus Jesus had arrived at Bethany April 4, which was a Friday. His meal with Lazarus at Bethany must have been a Sabbath meal. That means "the next day" could not have been the Sabbath, when Jesus and His disciples would have rested, but instead, Sunday, April 6, 32 C.E.

The question is, was Sunday April 6, 32 C.E. exactly 173,880 days from Artaxerxes' decree on March 14, 445 B.C.E.? By counting we can discover that, in terms of the Julian calendar by which we operate, it is 477 years and 24 days. However, we must deduct one year because there was no year "0" between 1 B.C.E. and 1 C.E. There remains 476 years and 24 days which amounts to 173,764 days (476x 365 +24 = 173,764).

Leap years add 119 days to that (476 divided by 4 =119), which brings us to 173,883 days. That is remarkably close to the 173,880 days we figured in Daniel, but not exactly the same. Anderson notes that the Julian calendar is still slightly inaccurate to the true solar year. The measure of this imprecision is 1/128. That is, the Julian calendar year is 1/128 of a day longer than a true solar year. We then omit leap years every 128 years on our calendar. During a period of 483 years, as in Daniel's sixty-nine weeks, there are three such omissions. So we may subtract three days from our total and arrive at precisely the same number with which we began, 173,880.

We can now figure Daniel's seventy weeks less one to the exact day that Jesus entered Jerusalem on the back of a donkey. Daniel also speaks of the anointed one's (Hebrew Mashiach, or Messiah) being cut off.

The Hebrew term yakaret implies a sudden, violent end, which conforms to Jesus' crucifixion.

Not only was it prophesied that Yeshua would ride into Jerusalem on a donkey, but, it is awesome that the exact date was also prophesied and fulfilled.

Following that it states, "the people of the prince who is to come" will destroy the city and the sanctuary. This conforms to the unprecedented destruction wrought upon Jerusalem by the Roman Legions of Titus in 70 C.E.

*　*　*

Scott studied this prophecy and its fulfillment over and over again. He marveled at its interpretation that could only be from the Word of God and His Plan.

Chapter XXXII

WHEN THE FOLLOWING Saturday arrived, Scott and Paige attended *Sabbath* services for the second time at the Chiam B' Derech Synagogue in Russellville. Again, he was greeted by the leaders of this house of worship, Randy and Beth Cook. They made both he and Paige feel very special, as if, it was an honor for them to receive them. Scott looked around this humble congregation made up of different races and nationalities who conducted themselves as one big family worshipping their Messiah, Yeshua.

Scott, who had trouble understanding the Hebrew language, noticed that their prayer book had an English translation next to the Hebrew. He asked himself why he did not notice this the last time he attended and he realized that he wasn't open-minded enough, because he was dwelling on the past, when he felt inadequate as to knowing the Hebrew language in an Orthodox environment. Yes, this is an Orthodox Messianic Synagogue observing all holidays, wearing *yamikas*, and *talisis'*(prayer shawls) and some of the men even wearing *tallit katan* (a fringed garment traditionally worn by Orthodox Jewish men under or over their clothing). Some, if not all of the members of this congregation, kept *kosher* (observing the Jewish Dietary Laws).

Scott observed that most of the congregation were not born and raised Jewish. These were Gentiles who wanted to learn about their Jewish roots and worship Yeshua in the way He is most likely worshipped, as a Jewish Rabbi.

Scott went to Hebrew school for three years and could hardly understand the Hebrew that he read, yet these people had taken the time and opportunity to read and understand Hebrew. He admired them.

Going forward, he realized it was necessary for him to change some of his ways and embrace his own Jewish roots.

At one point, during the service, there were prayer requests and praise reports and Paige took this opportunity to publicly thank Yeshua for bringing Scott through his life threatening illness.

When the service had ended, he shook hands with Randy and left with a very positive attitude.

Chapter XXXIII

Scott was nearing the end of his spiritual quest and he felt that the Lord had guided him to Russellville to join Paige and her family, in order for him to find Yeshua and for them to become aware of their Jewish roots.

Paige had a large family and this was a bonus for Scott in his retirement years. He laughed with them, cried with them and he prayed with them and for them.

He remembered the time Paige's grandson, Chris was having a difficult time finding himself and going through a horrible divorce with child custody issues. Scott prayed that Chris would find peace in his life and it came in the form of his son, Haiden. He took that boy almost everywhere he went. Scott believed that Haiden was the light in Chris' eyes that made him smile and find peace.

When Paige's grandson Tyler, who has a beautiful voice, decided to try out for American Idol, Scott prayed that he would be picked, but after two attempts, he thought maybe the third would be a charm.

Her granddaughter, Taylor, was nine years old when Scott moved to Russellville and she reminded him of his daughter, Tommy, who was the same age the last time he saw her. Taylor acted as Tommy's proxy as he watched her grow up.

In addition to Paige's family, Scott knew that he hit the jackpot when he married Paige. She was always there for him and their love would be served.

And during all of this, Risky was always there. When Scott sneezed and if Paige cried, he was always in their faces to make sure they were alright. Throughout all of the shoes and dishtowels that he could steal, his love remained unconditional.

In the beginning, Scott felt that it would be impossible for him to be completely happy in Russellville. After all, he was educated in New York City and traveled and lived throughout the world; so how could he be happy in a small place like this? But, now he found an inner peace living here and couldn't imagine living anywhere else. He now considered this peaceful little city to be his home and his heaven on earth.

* * *

For Scott, the evidence that Yeshua is the Messiah was overwhelming. Not only did he read, understand and believe that the prophecies and their fulfillment concerning Yeshua were ironclad, but Yeshua had personally come into his life.

Yeshua came to Scott in a dream when Paige asked Jason Crabb to pray for him and his prayer was for Jesus to reveal himself to Scott. Yeshua returned Risky to Scott. Yeshua presented himself to Scott in a vision. Yeshua used Scott as his instrument to help Fred Morris find salvation. Yeshua healed his Crohn's disease, which is incurable. On Easter Sunday, Yeshua signaled Scott through his body, that something was wrong with his hip, which turned into a life-threatening event. He also believed that Yeshua guided him to the Complete Jewish Bible, which introduced him to Messianic Judaism.

Throughout everything that happened up this point, Scott still had tremendous feelings of guilt regarding his acceptance of Messianic Judaism. At times he felt like he was back in a casino again flipping a coin with mainstream Judaism on one side and Messianic Judaism on the other and he was waiting for it to land to see the outcome. But, this coin did not land on its side, rather on its edge and remained there. Even a strong wind could not persuade it to lose its balance and land one way or the other. It remained steadfast on its edge; thus, combining the best of Judaism and Christianity equaling Messianic Judaism.

Scott knew that finally he made a bet in his life that won.

Chapter XXXIV

SCOTT NOW FELT comfortable whether he visited a Messianic Synagogue or the First Assembly of God Church.

On one Sunday morning, his past came full circle when he attended the morning service at the First Assembly of God Church in Russellville.

As the service was drawing to a close, he started to sweat and he felt his heart beating like drum in his chest, as Pastor Ronnie Morris said, "Is there anyone here who has not yet accepted Jesus as their personal Savior and wants to now, please come forward."

At that moment, Scott knew that he did not have to come forward, because he was convinced that Yeshua was his Messiah and personal Savior. He was proud to be in the congregation of the First Assembly of God Church as a representative of Messianic Judaism.

His journey was now over and his quest was completed, as he had found the real Messiah, Yeshua.

Scott, Paige & Risky

Scott & Risky

OTHER NOVELS

By
Stanley Cohen

The Risk Taker

A Chip And A Chair

To learn more about these novels and where to purchase them, visit:

www.therisktakerbooks.com

www.ingramcontent.com/pod-product-compliance
Lightning Source LLC
Chambersburg PA
CBHW021116080526
44587CB00010B/541